living WITH *dying*

Edited by Helen Alexander

Credits

Published 1990 by Broadcasting Support
Services to accompany **Living with Dying**,
a series first shown on BBC television in
February and March 1990

ISBN 0 906965 36 5

Edited by
Helen Alexander

Cover design by
Dick Bailey

Book design by
GIDA Design Consultants

Printed by
Haynes Cannon Ltd

Distributed by
Broadcasting Support Services

The publication of this book has been assisted
by a grant from PFG Hodgson Kenyon
International plc.

Broadcasting Support Services
provides follow – up services for
viewers and listeners.

For further copies please send a cheque or
postal order for £2.75, payble to BSS, to
Living with Dying, PO Box 7, London
W3 6XJ.

Contents

Foreword

When the BBC asked if I would like to present a documentary series about bereavement, my first instinct was to say no. After all, there is something intensely personal about the loss of a loved one; everyone reacts in their own unique, private way, and what is right for one person might be wholly wrong for another. There is no set formula for grieving, and it was this absence of universal rules, combined with the nature and intensity of the emotions involved, that prompted my early doubts. I was also unsure whether it was an appropriate subject for television at all.

But as the doubts and arguments churned around in my mind, I realised that they were themselves a variation on the fears, the phobias and hang-ups – the almost perverse logic which has conditioned and coloured our national attitude towards bereavement over generations. The very nature of death and bereavement has made them immune to the normal thought processes and frank discussions that condition and shape every other aspect of our lives. We put death on a distant pedestal, revere it, fear it, prefer to ignore it until those rela-tively rare moments when it touches a loved one or colleague – thus creating around it an aura of isolation that deprives us of help when we need it most. With almost any other subject in an evolving, free society, such an attitude would have been questioned and challenged long ago. And yet, with death we con-tinue to make it peculiarly difficult for ourselves. The 20th century – so progressive in so many other ways – is leaving us an unwelcome legacy of constraints, taboos, often walls of silence enveloping death and the grief that goes with it. How strange when you think that death is life's one great certainty, something we *know* is going to happen to us all. And yet most of us don't talk about it, plan for it, acknowledge it in any way, until it is upon us – as though *not thinking about it* will somehow stop it happening. Life seems to be the only journey we make during which we prefer not to think about what will happen when we reach our destination!

However, like most busy people, such thoughts could easily have passed me by – if I had not been touched by the Hospice movement, which has long identified the extent of help that is needed not just for the dying, but for those they leave behind. Their specially trained counsellors go out of their way to prepare people for the death of a loved one, and offer them back-up, help, support and friendship for as long afterwards as it is needed. The existence of such dedicated people – and of a whole raft of other charities offering counselling and help to those who have been bereaved – is a powerful testament to a great and growing need. One relatively new charity was set up specifically to help those who had lost a child. Its existence was first revealed in a brief radio interview; that the charity's phone didn't stop ringing for *four days* as bereaved parents rang from all over Britain proved that *their* need was overwhelming.

But the fact is that *everyone* who dies leaves behind someone with a need for help. A few bereaved relatives appear to cope in an enviably self-contained way; most are not able to do so. The television series – like this book – is for that great majority, charting the pitfalls on a hugely emotional journey, showing the important practical steps that can be taken; above all, thinking of those who will be left behind, and offering them advice that may shape the course and length of what no – one denies is a deeply emotional voyage.

If, like me, you have ever watched the people you love die – suddenly or slowly – you will know the way emotions can tumble over each other to depress, frighten and confuse. At such a time, you will have known the importance of a shoulder to lean on, but you may also have been aware that friends and relatives, acting with the very best of intentions, often unwittingly said and did all the wrong things. Grief is personal and private. I cannot say with certainty that this book will be right for everyone, but I strongly believe it will help. It draws on a deep well of experience. The warm and fine words that follow are the considered thoughts and experiences of the professional counsellors and experts who gave us such good advice in the making of the television programmes. They are words that deserve a wider audience – and when you have read them you will understand why, after my early doubts, I said yes to presenting a television series on a subject most people run away from. Those words –and the testimony of the extraordinary people I had the privilege of interviewing – have undoubtedly given me a much more practical, positive approach to the whole subject of death and dying. I hope they will break some of the taboos for you too.

Martyn Lewis
February 1990

Making a will

Who wants to think about dying?

Nobody really wants to think about their own death, and so making a will tends to be pushed to the back of the mind. Sometimes people believe they have nothing worth leaving or that their money will go anyway to those whom they would want to receive it. These are both misconceptions.

If you think about it logically, who do you want to decide the eventual destination of all your worldly goods: yourself or the state? If you die intestate, that is, without making a will, the law will automatically decide what will happen to your estate and there will be no consideration at all of what your wishes might have been.

When you make a will, you are not tempting providence; you are merely expressing a desire about how you would like your assets to be divided. You can also use a will to protect your family or your partner (especially if you are living with someone outside a legally recognised partnership, in which case he or she may not be legally entitled to a penny), or to make donations to charity. Making a will ensures that your wishes regarding your estate are observed.

Another common concern about making a will is cost; yet drawing up a will is among the cheapest services a solicitor can provide, and the cost (normally around £50 but check first) is small when compared to the peace of mind you should feel. People on a low income may be able to get free or low-cost advice about wills from solicitors who display the legal aid sign.

What happens if I don't make a will?

If you die intestate, your estate (after all debts and liabilities have been paid) is divided among members of your family according to the strict rules laid down by the Administration of Estates Act (see Diagram 1).

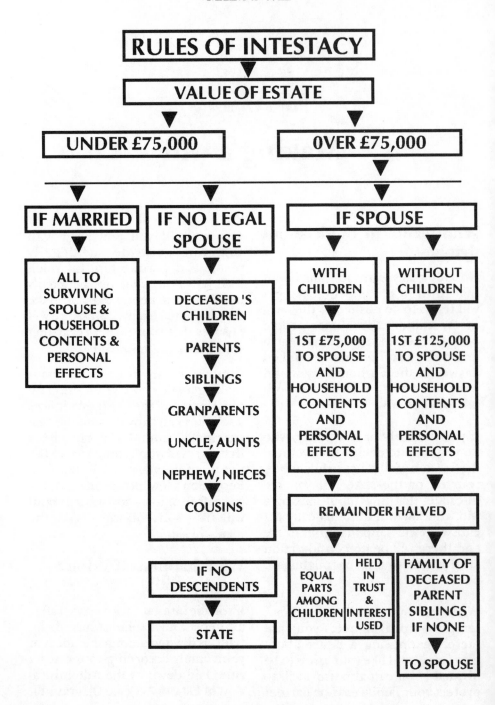

RULES OF INTESTACY

VALUE OF ESTATE

UNDER £75,000

OVER £75,000

IF MARRIED

ALL TO SURVIVING SPOUSE & HOUSEHOLD CONTENTS & PERSONAL EFFECTS

IF NO LEGAL SPOUSE

DECEASED 'S CHILDREN

PARENTS

SIBLINGS

GRANPARENTS

UNCLE, AUNTS

NEPHEW, NIECES

COUSINS

IF NO DESCENDENTS

STATE

IF SPOUSE

WITH CHILDREN

WITHOUT CHILDREN

1ST £75,000 TO SPOUSE AND HOUSEHOLD CONTENTS AND PERSONAL EFFECTS

1ST £125,000 TO SPOUSE AND HOUSEHOLD CONTENTS AND PERSONAL EFFECTS

REMAINDER HALVED

EQUAL PARTS AMONG CHILDREN	HELD IN TRUST & INTEREST USED

FAMILY OF DECEASED PARENT SIBLINGS IF NONE

TO SPOUSE

This applies to anyone whose domicile (real and permanent home) is in England or Wales.

Under these rules your surviving partner or family may have to sell your family home in order to pay other family members their entitlements.

If you die unmarried without any relatives and without a will, everything you own will go to the state.

If you are married

If the value of everything you own is less than £75,000, everything will go to your spouse, irrespective of children. If you own your home jointly then your share will automatically go to your spouse and it will not count as part of the estate.

If the value exceeds £75,000, things are more complicated. Your spouse still gets the first £75,000 as well as personal posessions. The rest is divided into two equal parts, one of which goes to your children to be equally divided. They will receive it at the age of 18. The second half goes into a trust and provides an income for your spouse. This capital, however, cannot be touched, although the interest can be used as income. It will ultimately go to the children on the death of your spouse.

If you have no children

Your spouse will receive the first £125,000 plus personal effects and one half of the remainder. The other half will go to your parents if they survive you; if not, it will go to your brothers and sisters or their children.

If you have no legal partner

All of the property will go equally to your children first of all or, if there are none, to a succession of your relatives (if they are dead, their children automatically assume their place) in this descending order of priority.

Parents
Brothers and sisters
Grandparents
Uncles and aunts
Nephews and nieces
Cousins

If you have no relatives, then all your estate will go to the Crown.

Other advantages of making a will

Even if you think that under these rules your property will go to whom you wish, it is of course impossible to guess in which order the deaths of a husband and wife will occur. Because of this, it is quite likely that if there is no will, the property will not go to the people you might have assumed. Also, your financial position may change.

If a husband and wife die together,

children under 18 are only able to receive the interest on the capital investment and there are restrictions on the kinds of investments which may be made, thus further restricting the possible interest available.

The chief advantages of making a will are as follows.

1. You can appoint an executor to distribute your property.

2. You can leave specific bequests to people or charities which would not benefit under the rules of intestacy (for instance, co-habitees or gay partners).

3. You ensure relative simplicity in dealing with personal property.

4. You can indicate your wishes about the type of funeral you want and donations of your organs or body.

5. You can appoint guardians for children under 18.

D-I-Y wills

Wills do not have to be drawn up by solicitors. You can buy a pre-printed form in a stationers, but they can be misleading or inappropriate for your particular circumstances. If you are going to do it yourself, make sure it is done properly. A badly drawn-up will could lead to long court cases and a reduction in the amount going to your beneficiaries.

Common mistakes made by people drawing up their own wills are:

1. failure to dispose of all assets, leading to partial intestacy;

2. non-witnessed alterations;

3. failure to consider the possibility of a beneficiary dying before a testator;

4. failure to consider the effects of testator's remarriage/divorce;

5. being unaware of your dependants' rights to claim if reasonable financial provision is not made for them;

6. failure to have the will properly signed and witnessed.

You should only attempt to draw up your own will if your circumstances are fairly straightforward, and if you really cannot afford to have a solicitor do it for you.

Making your will

Anyone can make a will if they are over 18 with 'testamentary capacity'. A will usually has three distinct sections:

1. appointment of executors, guardians of children, funeral wishes, etc.;

2. distribution of property;

3. administrative provision.

First things to think about

1. Choose a solicitor.

2. Assess the value of your estate. Calculate roughly what your assets are worth, then deduct what debts and liabilities you have. The result

is your net estate. (It may be helpful to draw a chart similar to the one on the following page.)

3. Decide on the beneficiaries: spouse/partner/children/grand-children/other relatives/friends/ charities

4. Appoint executors and talk to them about it.

A *Personal Assets Log* form has been prepared by the Law Society and can be obtained from The Bookshop, The Law Society, 113 Chancery Lane, London WC2A 1PL.

Points to bear in mind

Let your executors know where your will is; sometimes it is easier to keep it at home as there may be a delay getting it out of a bank. It is helpful to keep a list of your assets with your will and regularly update it – your aim should be to make things as easy as possible for your executors.

Bear in mind that your will only comes into operation after your death. You can alter your will at any time up till then. Alterations should not be made to the will other than by codicil, a supplement modifying a will, or they will not be legally valid.

If circumstances change too much, it is better to make a completely new will and revoke the previous one. It is best to destroy the previous one to avoid later confusion.

Marriage and divorce

If you get married after you have drawn up your will, then your will is automatically revoked. If you do not draw up a new will, you will be deemed as intestate when you die.

However, the will is *not* revoked if you get divorced. What happens is that your former spouse cannot act as executor and cannot benefit from the will. Again, it is always best to draw up a new will.

Finally, wills should be reviewed every two or three years, just to make sure they are up-to-date.

Making things easy for those you leave behind

The most useful and practical thing you can do for your family is to leave behind a list of everything they will need to know upon your death. You can easily compile the relevant information by following the guidelines suggested in the two checklists entitled 'People to inform' and 'Documents' (pages 7 and 8).

If all this information is easily available to your family, all the necessary arrangements can be sorted out very quickly and a lot of heartache can be avoided.

Funeral arrangements and organ donation

If you have any specific wishes regarding your funeral and or organ

YOUR ASSETS

House present value	£	Furniture	£
Car	£	Household effects	£
Savings & cash	£	Jewellery	£
Stocks & shares	£	Clothing	£
Insurance policies	£	Anything else of value	£
Pension benefits	£		
Bank & building society accounts	£	**TOTAL**	£

YOUR LIABILITIES

Mortgage	£	Other debts	£
Bank loan	£	Tax owed	£
HP agreements	£		
Credit card debts	£	**TOTAL**	£

donation, it is wise to leave a note clearly setting out your wishes somewhere very obvious in case your will does not come to light for a few days. Always ensure your partner/ spouse knows your wishes too.

Your executor

Your will should name an executor, that is, someone, normally close to you, who will administer your estate, following the instructions in your will.

If you are in the position of being an executor, you will have to apply for a Grant of Probate which confirms the executor's entitlement to deal with the estate and formally recognises the will in the local Probate Registry. In the case of intestacy, someone will have to apply for Letters of Administration. There are rules about who may initially apply for these and they simply grant you the authority to administer the estate, which means paying the deceased's bills and dealing out the remainder to the beneficiaries. The Probate Registry normally requires a search for a will to be undertaken before intestacy is accepted. If the estate comes to less than £5,000, it may be possible for it to be released without either of the above. Unless the estate is very small (under £5,000), banks and insurance companies are unlikely to pay out on any policies without seeing the probate document. The Probate Registry will also be able to tell you if it is likely that any inheritance tax will have to be paid. If the estate is large (more than £118,000), you will need a solicitor.

Being an executor means you are now the personal representative of the deceased. Your job is simply to carry out his/her wishes to the best of your ability and to pay any debts or taxes arising from the will. Do not forget that until the funeral bill is paid, the deceased is still incurring expenditure and that these costs too should be met by the estate. Occasionally, it is advisable to advertise for creditors so that you can be sure of having done your best to settle all debts. It is important to keep a note of every expenditure as such things as telephone calls, taxis for mourners and clothes for the funeral are all tax deductible.

You can refuse to be an executor, but it is advisable to read the will first, and do not forget that you can be providing an invaluable service and support not only to the deceased, but also to those family members and friends left behind.

MAKING A WILL

SUGGESTED FORMAT FOR
'PEOPLE TO INFORM' CHECKLIST

	NAME / ADDRESS / TEL NO
EMPLOYER	
ACCOUNTANT	
SOLICITOR	
STOCKBROKER	
CAR INSURANCE CO	
POST OFFICE (if a/c held)	
BUILDING SOCIETY	
BANK	
PENSION GROUP	
LIFE INSURERS	
HOME INSURANCE (CONTENTS) CO	
HOME INSURANCE (BUILDINGS) CO	
TAX OFFICE	
EXECUTORS OF WILL	
CREDIT CARD CO	
CLUBS/SOCIETIES	
AA/RAC	
SOCIAL SERVICES	
SOCIAL SECURITY OFFICE	
HOSPITAL	
GP	
TRADE UNION	
TEACHER (if child involved)	
GAS BOARD	
ELECTRICITY BOARD	
TELEPHONE COMPANY	
DVLC	
LANDLORD	
SCHOOL/COLLEGE	

DOCUMENT CHECKLIST

DOCUMENT	LOCATION
WILL	
BIRTH/MARRIAGE CERTIFICATE	
*PASSPORT	
LIFE ASSURANCE POLICY	
CAR INSURANCE POLICY	
HOME CONTENTS POLICY	
HOUSE BUILDING POLICY	
SHARES/INVESTMENTS CERTIFICATES	
DISABILITY POLICIES	
MORTGAGE PAPERS	
PROPERTY DEEDS	
PREMIUM BONDS	
UNIT TRUSTS	
NATIONAL SAVINGS CERTIFICATES	
BANK ACCOUNT BOOKS	
CHEQUEBOOKS	
OTHER ACCOUNT BOOKS (Building Society/ Post Office)	
PENSION DETAILS	
* CREDIT CARDS	
* MEMBERSHIP CARDS	
FUNERAL PLANS	
PROVISION FOR FUNERAL EXPENSES	
* DRIVING LICENCE	
* ORDER BOOKS (Child benefit, etc.)	
* CAR REGISTRATION DOCUMENTS	
* SEASON TICKETS	
* LIBRARY TICKETS	
* N.I. PAPERS	
* MEDICAL CARD	

The documents above which are marked with an asterisk (*) should be returned to the relevant authority by the executor.

What happens after a death ?

When someone dies there are quite a number of things that have to be done and only a short time in which to do them.

If a friend or a member of your family offers to come and stay with you, accept the offer because you will need support. It is also a great help if you can find someone who will take on the burden of paperwork.

Death in the home

If someone dies in your home expectedly after an illness, there are a few people who need to be told; however, this does not have to happen immediately. There is time for you and your family to say goodbye. Also, you do not have to ring a doctor up in the middle of the night. If you feel you can cope on your own, wait until the morning. Your doctor will appreciate it.

The people you need to tell are:

—the doctor who was in attendance;

– the nearest relatives.

Even if you have lapsed from any religious faith, do not hesitate to contact a minister, priest or other religious representative if you want to. He or she should be able to provide emotional and spiritual support. After that, you will have to think about finding a funeral director. He will be able to relieve you of a lot of the practical burdens. Your doctor or minister may be able to help you to find someone. Also at this stage, you will have to start thinking about whether the body is to be buried or cremated. The funeral director will need to know as soon as possible as an additional form has to be signed by a second doctor if there is to be a cremation.

Do not forget that you have the choice of keeping the body at home until the funeral. Some people find this very helpful.

If someone dies unexpectedly in the home, then you must inform

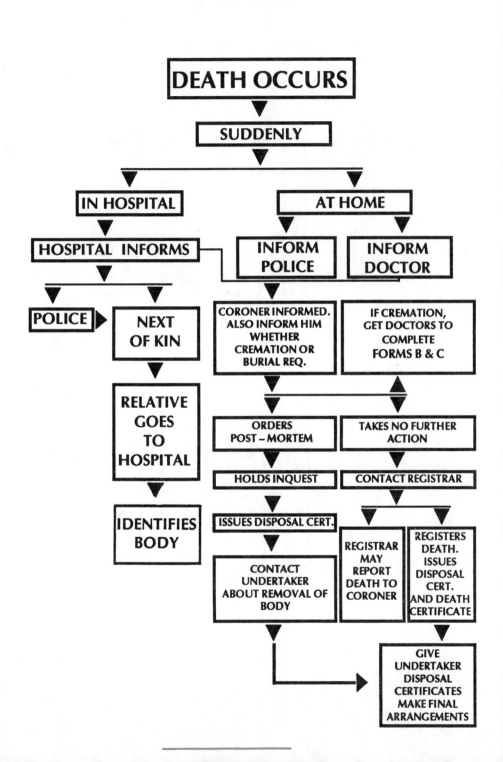

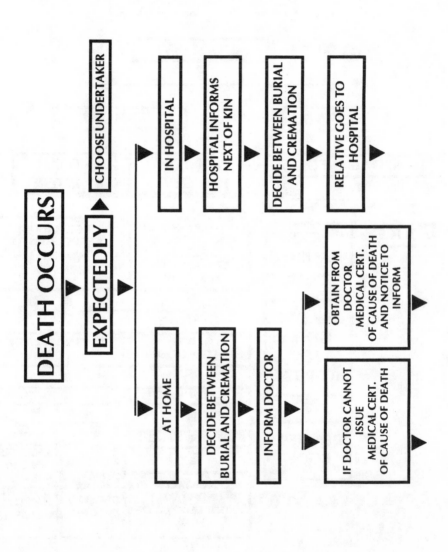

DEATH OCCURS ▶ **EXPECTEDLY** ▶ CHOOSE UNDERTAKER

IN HOSPITAL ▶ HOSPITAL INFORMS NEXT OF KIN ▶ DECIDE BETWEEN BURIAL AND CREMATION ▶ RELATIVE GOES TO HOSPITAL ▶

AT HOME ▶ DECIDE BETWEEN BURIAL AND CREMATION ▶ INFORM DOCTOR ▶

OBTAIN FROM DOCTOR MEDICAL CERT. OF CAUSE OF DEATH AND NOTICE TO INFORM ▶

IF DOCTOR CANNOT ISSUE MEDICAL CERT. OF CAUSE OF DEATH ▶

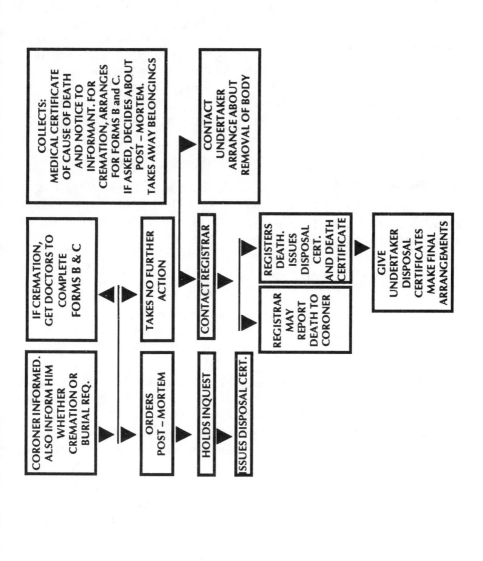

CORONER INFORMED. ALSO INFORM HIM WHETHER CREMATION OR BURIAL REQ.

IF CREMATION, GET DOCTORS TO COMPLETE FORMS B & C

COLLECTS: MEDICAL CERTIFICATE OF CAUSE OF DEATH AND NOTICE TO INFORMANT. FOR CREMATION, ARRANGES FOR FORMS B and C. IF ASKED, DECIDES ABOUT POST – MORTEM. TAKES AWAY BELONGINGS

CONTACT UNDERTAKER ARRANGE ABOUT REMOVAL OF BODY

TAKES NO FURTHER ACTION

ORDERS POST – MORTEM

CONTACT REGISTRAR

HOLDS INQUEST

REGISTRAR MAY REPORT DEATH TO CORONER

REGISTERS DEATH. ISSUES DISPOSAL CERT. AND DEATH CERTIFICATE

ISSUES DISPOSAL CERT.

GIVE UNDERTAKER DISPOSAL CERTIFICATES MAKE FINAL ARRANGEMENTS the police as well as a doctor. This may seem harsh, but unexpected death does have to be investigated.

Death in a hospital

If someone dies after an illness in hospital, the ward sister will tell the next of kin. If the death is as a result of an accident, then she will have to inform the police and a relative will have to identify the body.

Organ donation

If the person who has died has expressed a wish that their organs should be used for transplant, the authorities will need to know speedily. Because of time considerations, transplant is only possible when the death occurs in a hospital. If the death is sudden (particularly, for example, the accidental death of the young), you may be asked for permission to remove organs whether or not the deceased has expressed this wish. Organ transplantation can help save other lives and can be a considerable source of comfort to you.

Medical certificate of cause of death

This is necessary for all deaths. It is a certificate filled in by a doctor stating the cause of death. The doctor can only issue it if he/she is confident about the cause of death, and in any case, he/she must have seen the deceased within the previous 14 days (28 in Northern Ireland). It will be given to the next of kin by the GP or by a doctor in the hospital. There is no charge. If the body is to be cremated, then two forms (B and C) will have to be completed by two doctors. (In the case of cremation the cause of death must be certain, since the body cannot be exhumed afterwards.)

Notice to informant

The medical certificate will be given to you in a sealed envelope, addressed to the registrar along with the 'notice to informant'. The informant is simply the person who goes to register the death. This person can be one of several:

1. A relative who was present at the death or during the illness or one who lives in the district of the registrar;

2. Anyone who was present at the death, or was living in the house and knew about it;

3. The occupier of the house, or the senior resident officer of the institution, in which the death occurred;

4. The person making the funeral arrangements;

5. Any person having knowledge of the particulars required (Scotland only);

6. The deceased's executor or legal representative (Scotland only).

Registering a death

You have to do this within five days (eight in Scotland) in the Registry Office covering the area in which the death took place (or, in Scotland, where the deceased normally resided). Sadly, you cannot make an appointment, and you may have to wait a long time, so take a friend with you.

The registrar will need a certain amount of information. It helps if you take along:

1.The medical certificate of cause of death and notice to informant;

2.The medical card, birth and marriage certificate of the deceased.

Other facts the registrar will want to know about the deceased are these.

1.Full name and address.

2.Date and place of birth and death.

3.Occupation

4.If female and married, maiden name, and name and occupation of husband.

5.If under 16, full names and occupations of parents.

6.Whether there was a pension or allowance from public funds

In Scotland the registrar will also want to know the following.

1.Time of death.

2. If deceased had ever been married.

3. Names and occupations of parents and whether they are still living.

When the registrar has all the information, he will prepare a draft entry to the register, which you will have to check and sign.

The registrar will give you:

1. A certificate for burial or cremation (green form) which should be given to the funeral director (not in Scotland) (a body cannot be cremated or buried without this so it is unwise to make final funeral arrangements until you have it);

2. A certificate of registration of death (white form);

3. He should also be able to provide DSS leaflets so that you can check if you are entitled to any benefits.

The death certificate

This certificate confirms the registration of the death. You will need it:

1. to claim any benefits;

2. to apply for a Grant of Probate or Letters of Administration;

3. to claim life assurance/insurance.

If for any reason the registration has to be delayed, then the registrar can provide you with various interim certificates. Take along with you a list of the purposes for which you think evidence of death may be required and the registrar will advise you. Do not forget that although the original death certificate is free, you will be charged for copies and for some of the interim certificates. You can also get copies from the main registry offices in London, Edinburgh or Belfast.

The coroner (procurator fiscal in Scotland)

In some cases a medical certificate of cause of death cannot be issued, for instance if a doctor had not attended the deceased during his last illness or seen him during the last 14 days (28 in Northern Ireland). Such deaths have to be reported to a coroner. Other deaths which have to be reported to the coroner are these.

1. Death during an operation or within 24 hours of one

2. Sudden, inexplicable, accidental or suspicious death

3. Death due to neglect, poisoning, drugs, abortion or suicide

4. Death attributable to industrial disease

5. Death caused by or accelerated by injuries received during military service.

The job of the coroner is simply to look into any death reported to him and to decide whether further in-

vestigation is needed. If he decides that no further action is needed, he sends notice of his decision to the registrar and the death is registered in the normal way by the informant.

If the coroner decides that further investigation is necessary, the death cannot be registered, but he can issue an interim certificate of death so that dealings with the deceased's estate can be set in motion.

It is important to bear in mind that just because the coroner has been informed, the investigation will not necessarily end in a post-mortem or inquest. In the majority of cases, the involvement of the coroner is a formality.

Post-mortems

Post-mortems can happen in two ways. A hospital can ask the family's permission for a post-mortem to be carried out for several reasons, for example if the person was in hospital for a short period of time or if the doctors wish to know more about the cause of death. In this instance, the family can refuse.

The second way is that a coroner can order a post-mortem to establish the cause of death. This may be to show the death was a natural one or it may resolve a dispute. Sometimes, a post-mortem provides evidence if there has been a criminal death. In this case, the family do not have to be asked for permission.

They can, however, raise any religious objections, which will be taken into consideration.

Do not forget you can ask for a doctor of your choosing to be present at the post-mortem.

The coroner has no obligation to tell the family the result of a post-mortem. You will have to inquire at the coroner's office to find out if the notification has gone to the registrar for the death certificate to be issued. It may be that the registrar will contact the next of kin when he receives notice from the coroner.

In either case, the death still has to be registered by the informant.

Inquests (public inquiry in Scotland)

An inquest is merely an inquiry to determine who the deceased person was and how, when and where he or she died. A coroner is obliged to hold an inquest into every violent or unnatural death reported to him. The inquest is held formally and is open to the public. It is a court of law and has the power to summon witnesses and jurors, but it is quite often held in a small room with the minimum of ceremony. The coroner sums up and gives his verdict after he has heard all the evidence. The conclusion has to be proven, otherwise an open verdict will be returned. An inquest does not determine criminal or civil liabilities. Do not forget that you can have a lawyer to represent your point of view. This may be important if death was a result of a road accident or an accident at work. Unfortunately, you cannot get legal aid for this, but there are solicitors who can provide invaluable help for specific types of cases, such as deaths arising out of medical accidents. It is certainly worth looking into this if you feel that you need this kind of help.

After the inquest the coroner sends a certificate to the registrar and the death is registered. There is no need for an informant to attend and the family can obtain a copy of the death certificate from the registrar.

Arranging the funeral

If you are in the position of having to arrange a funeral, you should find out, unless you already know, if the deceased left any specific instructions. However, there is no *legal* obligation to carry out a dead person's wishes in this respect. If there are no guidelines, then the decision whether to bury or to cremate is usually made by the next of kin or the executor.

Funeral directors

There is a National Association of Funeral Directors (NAFD; for address, see Appendix 1) and they have drawn up a code of practice for dealing with the public. Members must give information about services and prices, and provide a written estimate and a detailed account. They must offer a basic simple funeral if that is all that is required.

A funeral director's job is to be responsible for organising the funeral and to provide what is necessary. These are as follows.

1. Make any necessary preparations to the body.

2. Arrange for the removal of the body to a chapel (if that is what you wish).

3. Schedule and organise the funeral with the cemetery or crematorium.

4. Liaise with clergy, organist and others and make payments.

5. Advise on registration of death.

6. Check you have all the necessary documents and that all the official forms have been completed.

Paying for the funeral

Find out first of all if any provision for paying for the funeral has been made. There may be a prepaid plan or an insurance policy which will pay for it. The funeral is usually paid for out of the estate. If money is limited, tell the undertaker how much you are prepared to spend and find out what he can offer you for that sum. You can get quotes from several undertakers.

If you are claiming social security, you may be able to claim the whole cost or part of the cost of a basic funeral. Forms for this are available from the DSS.

Costs you will have to consider are the laying out of the body, the coffin, the removal of the body from the house or hospital, a shroud, extra cars (or mileage). Fees are payable to the church, cemetery or crematorium, and to the clergyman (or other person who takes the service) and organist if necessary. Costs can be anywhere from £400 to £1200.

It is important that you check with the funeral director whether in the area in which you live there is an agreement that the local authority provides a very low-cost funeral for residents. In London, borough councils already operating such a scheme are Islington, Hounslow, Lambeth and Lewisham. Many other local authorities are also looking into this.

Before the funeral

You must arrange for the funeral director to remove the body from the hospital or the home, or from the mortuary if there has been a post – mortem. If, on the other hand, the body is to remain in the house until the funeral, then the undertaker will arrange for someone to come and lay it out if it has not been done already. If the body is to be picked up from the hospital or mortuary, the undertaker will need the disposal certificate or written permission from a relative or executor. Most undertakers keep the body on their premises until the funeral, and this enables the relatives and friends to view the body. Some large firms have central storing places for bodies and so the small undertaker's office you originally visit may not be where the body will be kept. It is worth finding this out beforehand in case it involves travelling. Some funeral parlours also have chapels where services can be carried out before going to the cemetery or crematorium.

Forms of service

Explore the possibilities

Remember, a funeral is an opportunity to say goodbye to a loved one. After a funeral has passed, people may be left with the feeling that they were swept into a traditional 'off-the-peg' funeral and they may wish that they could have been more involved or had a more meaningful ceremony. If you feel you have said goodbye in an appropriate way, the process of mourning may be easier, so do not hesitate to talk to the person conducting the funeral about ways to make it more personal. (See also Part 2, Chapter 5.)

Non-religious ceremonies

There is no legal obligation that a particular type of person should perform a funeral service. Anyone

FUNERAL ARRANGEMENTS

▼

DECIDE WITH UNDERTAKER WHERE BODY AWAITES FUNERAL. DISCUSS EMBALMING

▼

CREMATION

▼

DECIDE ON CREMATORIUM MAKE PROVISIONAL BOOKING. CHOOSE COFFIN, COMPLETE CREMATORIUM'S FORM A

▼

GIVE CREMATORIUM AUTHORITIES: DISPOSAL CERTIFICATE FORM A, DOCTORS, FORMS B & C. CONFIRM: TIME OF CREMATION & ARRANGEMENTS E.G. USE OF CREMATORIUM CHAPEL

▼

DECIDE ABOUT DISPOSAL OF ASHES.

▼

SCATTER IN CREMATORIUM, CHURCHYARD OR ELSEWHERE BURY IN CHURCHYARD, CEMETERY OR ELSEWHERE KEEP IN URN IN CREMATURIUM, AT HOME OR ELSEWHERE

BURIAL

▼

CHURCHYARD

CEMETERY

▼

CHOOSE COFFIN, MAKE PROVISIONAL BOOKING

▼

GIVE CLERGY DISPOSAL CERTIFICATE. CONFIRM TIME OF FUNERAL. FOR A FACULTY GRAVE, SEND WRITTEN PROOF OF OWNERSHIP

GIVE CEMETERY AUTHORITIES DISPOSAL CERTIFICATE. CONFIRM TIME OF FUNERAL. CHOOSE TYPE & PLACE OF GRAVE: COMPLETE ANY APPLICATION FORM. FOR A PRIVATE GRAVE, SEND GRAVE DEEDS

▼

CONFIRM FINAL DETAILES WITH UNDERTAKER. ARRANGE AS REQUIRED: NOTICES IN PAPERS FLOWERS NUMBER OF CARS ORDER OF MOURNERS TIME AND STARTING POINT OF FUNERAL ARRANGEMENT AT END OF FUNERAL INCLUDING ANY REFRESHMENTS

IF SERVICE REQUIRED, ARRANGE WITH CLERGY TIME, PLACE AND TYPE OF SERVICE

▼

FUNERAL

can do it. If you do not want to have a religious service, you can have a ceremony with an officiant who will conduct it along the same lines as a minister would. Officiants can be members of the family, or close friends, a representative of an appropriate organisation or a sympathetic religious minister. It is advisable that the person conducting the ceremony should have some experience of handling meetings or some other appropriate experience. Advice can be sought from the following bodies.

1. British Humanist Association, 13 Prince of Wales Terrace, London W8 5PG.

2. National Secular Society, 702 Holloway Road, London N19 3NL.

3. Rationalist Press Association, 88 Islington High Street, London N1 8EW.

4. South Place Ethical Society, Conway Hall, 25 Red Lion Square, London WC1R 4RL

Please remember that whoever it is who takes the service, whether minister, friend or humanist officiant, they will want to be involved with you and your family as soon as they can in order to make the ceremony as positive and meaningful as possible.

Final arrangements for any funeral should not be confirmed until the disposal certificate has been obtained from the registrar, or the order for burial from the coroner.

Burial

Burials can take place in churchyards, where the vicar of the church allocates the site. But nowadays cemeteries are more usual. Most cemeteries are non-denominational and are run by a local authority or privately owned company. There may be consecrated parts within the cemetery, for which various extra fees apply for being buried there. There may also be ground dedicated to various specific faiths. Any kind of service can be held in a cemetery.

In a church service the mourners follow the coffin into the church, and the coffin is placed before the altar by the bearers. After the service, the bearers carry the coffin to the grave and the mourners follow. The coffin is lowered by the bearers into the grave as the words of committal are said. Sometimes the mourners throw handfuls of earth on top of the coffin. An entry is made in the burial register to show the burial has taken place.

There is no rule about fee-paying and each cemetery has its own scale of fees. There is usually a form to be filled in which must be returned along with all payments before the funeral takes place. There are different types of graves available in each cemetery and it is as well to check what is available.

If you want to be buried anywhere other than a churchyard or cemetery, the burial must be registered and usually you will have to apply for permission. There may also be health regulations.

Documents required

1. Registrar's certificate for burial or coroner's order.
2. Application for burial in cemetery.
3. Grave deeds or faculty.
4. Copy of entry in burial register. This proves the burial and locates the grave and is given by the burial authorities to the next of kin or executor.

Cremation

Cremation is impossible until the cause of death has been definitely established. This means it usually has to wait until the death has been registered or a coroner's certificate for cremation has been given.

Documents required

Four forms have to be completed, one by the next of kin, the other three by three different doctors. The forms can be issued by the crematorium, but the undertaker will have some and will help with their completion.

Form A is the application for crema-

tion, and must be filled in by the executor or next of kin.

Forms B and C are on the same piece of paper. Form B has to completed by the doctor who attended the deceased during his last illness, and he has to see the body before he can complete the form. On this form are details pertaining specifically to cremation which the doctor might have to find out from the family, for example, whether the deceased has a pacemaker.

Form C is the confirmatory medical certificate and must be completed by a doctor who has been registered as a medical practitioner in the UK for five years. This doctor must not be a relative of the deceased or of the doctor who completed form B. The second doctor also has to see the body.

Each doctor is entitled to a small fee for filling in the forms and there may also be a fee for removing a pacemaker prior to cremation. If death occurred in a hospital, then form C is not required if a post-mortem examination has already been carried out and the result is known to the doctor completing form B.

If the coroner has issued a certificate of cremation, then forms B and C are not needed. This means that if a death is reported to the coroner, you must let him know from the beginning if you want the body to be cremated so that the eventual authority to dispose of it will come in the appropriate format.

The final authority to cremate the body is given on form F which must be signed by a third doctor, the medical referee of the crematorium. He usually does this on the evidence of forms B and C or after he has received the coroner's certificate. If he is not satisfied by forms B and C, he has the power to refuse authority to cremate and can order a post-mortem or refer the matter to the coroner. The relatives of the deceased have no choice but to abide by this unless they opt for burial.

If the body of a stillborn child is to be cremated, then a special certificate has to be completed by the doctor who was present at the stillbirth and who examined the body. No second certificate is required. Form F must still be completed.

The purpose of all these forms is to ensure that no cremation can possibly take place unless every doubt has been removed as to the cause of death.

Most crematoria are run by local authorities and have their own scale of fees. Cremations do not take place at weekends and there may be an extra charge for a cremation out of normal working hours. The charge usually includes the use of the chapel, whether you use it or not.

If there is to be a service, it will either take place in a church beforehand or at the crematorium chapel. The coffin is carried in and placed on the catafalque. At the committal, the coffin is removed from the sight of the mourners, either by being moved mechanically or by having a curtain dropped in front of it. The coffin then goes into the committal room to await cremation. Each coffin is burnt individually. Each cremation is registered at the crematorium.

The ashes

Arrangements for the disposal of the ashes do not need to be made until after the cremation. They can be collected 24 hours afterwards or the crematorium will scatter or bury them for you. If you want to keep the ashes, undertakers can provide urns or caskets. There is no law regarding the disposal of ashes, which can be scattered anywhere. The crematorium will scatter them for you in their garden of remembrance. Ashes can also be buried in the consecrated ground of a churchyard or cemetery.

After the funeral

If there are to be any refreshments, make sure the mourners know where to go and that they have transport.

The undertaker will submit his bill which should be very detailed and which should show details of all payments he has made on your behalf. They are usually understanding about having to wait for payment until the deceased's affairs are sorted out. The charges an undertaker makes are not subject to VAT.

Benefits

If you are in any doubt about which benefits you might be entitled to, if any, there is a freephone Social Security number – 0800 666555. The person taking your call should be able to give you advice on Social Security and National Insurance. You should also get hold of the booklet published by the DSS entitled *What to Do After a Death?* which is stocked by all Citizens' Advice Bureaux.

There are various anomalies in the benefits. For instance, widows are entitled to a lump sum on the death of their husbands; but men receive no such sum on the death of their wives. Also, your entitlement to benefits depends largely on the NI contributions of yourself and your spouse, your age and your savings.

It might also be worthwhile to check your income tax allowance, as a widowed person can claim an extra single person's tax allowance to bring it up to a married person's allowance. Do not forget you may also be able to claim for housing benefit, guardian's allowance (if you take an orphan into your family) and various types of carers' and attendance allowances.

If you are in any doubt about your entitlement, **ask**, as most benefits do not come automatically.

'Just a few months'

The Rev. Tom Scott, Director, Strathcarron Hospice

'Just a few months...' That phrase, and the news it contains, can mean different things to different people. There is no 'best' way to hear the news – no 'best' way to make sense of it. There is your way: there is my way. There is each and every person's own way of living with dying.

It might help to think of it this way: just as being born is a unique event – unique to each person – so is the act of dying unique to each person. However, that does not mean the act of dying is an isolated event, that it is only happening to me. It has happened and will continue to happen to every mortal human being. 'Unique', yes, in that it is my death which I am facing – but 'alone', no, there are countless people who have been where I am now.

Perhaps we can look at and learn from the experience of others, not to copy their example, but to find, in the ways they have coped, things which make sense to us now, and

therefore things which will help. We put a great deal of time and thought into preparing for a birth; and in a similar way some people have the opportunity to prepare for their dying. The unexpected result of preparing for dying can be that a person's capacity for living will often be fuller than ever before.

But let us go back to the beginning. When we first hear bad news, very bad news, it often seems 'unbelievable'. So with part of me I do not believe it and I may actually deny to myself and to other people the fact that I only have some months left to live. And yet another part of me may have suspected for some time that there is something seriously wrong, something from which I am not getting better. The trouble is that the split between feeling 'this is unbelievable' and thinking 'this is what I have suspected' can cause confusion and anxiety. What can be done?

At this point we need someone who

will listen to us, who will allow us to put our half-thought questions into words, and who will answer the questions we ask. This may not all happen in one conversation. We may need two or three occasions to talk things through.

Usually the person who has the information we need is our doctor, particularly if he or she was the first person to say to us, 'You may have just a few months.' But the doctor needs our help too. It can make things much easier if we start the conversation and make it quite clear what it is we need: his or her time, listening ear, ability to answer the questions we ask. Reach an agreement to do just that. Remind him or her that the way we phrase our questions shows how much we want to take on at this particular point, and not to say more until we are ready to ask more the next time.

But what is the purpose of this business of asking questions and getting information? However unbelievable the news may be, we need to make sense of it. As we begin to make sense of it we can begin to dig deep into ourselves and find ways of coping, ways of facing the facts, ways of living with dying.

Frances, when she was first told at the age of 50 that she had a form of cancer, 'had a feeling of being ashamed and outcast as though I had been invaded by some horrible, hideous, evil force.' These feelings

came out in dreams. 'I used to dream I was covered in black spider-like crabs ... and I couldn't get them off my hands and body.' For Frances this was a terrible time of bad and difficult feelings, a time of being depressed and resentful as well as afraid.

'One day,' she wrote later, 'I was given a book written by a famous American doctor who said about cancer: "A cancer cell is in fact a weak and confused cell, a disorganised cell unable to perform its genetic functions." '

Frances described her reaction to reading those words 'I couldn't possibly continue to regard these poor weak things as an evil force, now could I? No. This helped me to realise that I am still indeed fearfully and wonderfully made and that the vast majority of my cells are still obeying their God-given DNA message. So I learned gradually to listen to my body, to rest when I need rest, but otherwise to function as normally as possible.'

Here we have one person's experience of how she made sense of what was happening, and how, having understood things better, she was able to be in far greater control of her life than she had first thought. In fact, Frances lived a very full life for nine more years.

However, that did not mean for Frances the end of feeling sad, or anxious, or really 'down'. Although we can grow in understanding about what is happening to us, nevertheless there are times when these negative feelings quite suddenly overwhelm us and threaten to take away those coping skills we have begun to discover within ourselves. Living with dying is sometimes not at all on an even keel.

Miranda had a way of dealing with such feelings. She saw herself as an oak tree, a strong and beautiful oak tree, threatened with a fungus which destroyed the leaves and weakened the branches. At the foot of the tree Miranda had powerful friends in a colony of ants. When she felt the fungus was winning the battle she called on the ants who went up the trunk of the oak tree, out along the branches and ate the fungus, so letting the leaves flourish again.

Miranda's way of understanding her situation and learning to cope with it was to see herself as battling with her disease. Certainly this image stood her in good stead for many months and it helped her to live as fully as possible.

When the time came for her to realise that she was losing the battle Miranda said that she found being an oak tree, something so strong and sturdy, was just too exhausting. She saw herself instead floating on an airbed in a gentle sun-kissed sea. With that new image she calmly came to the end of her life.

In both Frances and Miranda we see people able to go on making choices about their lives and the living of their lives. Illness may be bringing them to their dying, but it does not dominate their living.

'Just a few months...' One side of that phrase means the loss of everything. This can cause us to regret so much about the past. Some of the hurt we feel may never leave us because we feel we cannot put right some of the hurt we have caused to others. Frances was very aware of that and she said, 'It may sound odd but the first thing I had to do was to learn to love myself.' She meant she had to come to terms with the fact that in her life she had caused hurt to others, a truth she had to live with. Although she could not forget it, she came to see that it was not the whole truth about her. And so it no longer overwhelmed her. Just as she learned to live with the illness which afflicted her body, so she learned to live with herself, both her strengths and her weaknesses. As a result she found that she was still a person who could love herself – and others!

We can choose to look at the other side of the phrase. What can we do with 'just a few months'?

It is remarkable how much 'living' is done by people who know very well that the time left to them is measured in months or even weeks. All kinds of choices are possible:

fulfilling long-held ambitions to travel and visit particular places or people, trying your hand at painting or pottery, reading again books that are special. Far from finding life 'hopeless', people often learn to plan specific goals which may be fully achieved within the limits of the time that is left.

The time that is left can also be used for the fulfilling of the closest relationships. A man staying in a hospice asked his wife to bring in their family photo albums. Together they looked back to their wedding day; the arrival and growth of their children; family weddings; their first grandchild. In this way memories of the past enriched their last conversations together. Life had been full of rich experience and significant events. Life had been worth living.

A younger man was dying leaving his wife and three young children. They had only recently moved to the area. When he died should his wife and children move back to her native town or stay in their new home? Billy did not try to force a decision and died before the decision was made. But later when Irene had to make a decision about where she and her young ones were going to live she found it easier than she thought simply because she and Billy had shared the question together.

In each of these examples the people were able to find a sense of fulfilment. This is sometimes known as 'finishing unfinished business'. We can see that it is not just important for the person who is dying, but it is also important for those who are going to be bereaved. Being bereaved is a painful enough experience and sometimes there may be more suffering than there need be because of real regrets about things that were left unsaid or undone. So finishing unfinished business can ease the burden of bereavement in very practical and profound ways.

'Just a few months...' I suspect that most of us would live with this in both the ways I have described. Some of the time as we live with dying, the sense of loss and all the feelings which accompany that sense will be uppermost. At other times we will be able to use the time that is left as we choose. Perhaps the more we get used to the facts the easier it can be to cope with them.

However, in spite of learning to cope, many people have a sense of loneliness which can be hard to bear. People feel that there is no one who can understand, no one to listen, no one who will put up with my sighs of regret, my tears of sadness, or my outbursts of anger. But inevitably there are other people around. There may be family members, close friends, good neighbours, nurses and doctors, all of whom are accompanying the dying person in the last months and weeks of life. As time passes and as events take place some individuals, from among those who are in touch, may become special companions. They will become special because they are the kind of people who are easiest to relate to, and the kind of people who have what is needed most.

If I try to imagine myself with just a few months I think I can describe the kind of people I would like as my closest companions.

1. People who will somehow be there when I need them without making their presence felt all the time.

2. People who by the way they are will give me space and time, who will not crowd in on me, or try to move my thoughts on to other things because they find my thoughts difficult to take.

3. People who are safe to be with and with whom it is safe for me to be myself.

4. People who will tolerate my moods and tears and who will have the wisdom to know when to leave me in my moods and when to rescue me from them.

5. People who will let me take the lead, choose the path, set the pace when I can and who will lead me when I need to be led.

6. Someone most special with whom to say 'Goodbye' and 'I love you'.

But there are other people whose particular knowledge and skills I may need and want. They may come in and out of my life to do practical things like a doctor or a nurse, a bank manager to discuss financial matters, a solicitor to help in the making of a will. So there will be personal companions and practical companions, and sometimes companions who are both.

In the end, the person who is dying is coming to that event ahead of any of the companions. In the end, it is my death. Death has been called 'the last enemy', and a person may fight it all the way. For another it may be a longed-for liberation from all the pains that have been suffered, and such a person may welcome death. For another it may be an act of transformation, to new life with new dimensions, a step to be taken in trust and hope. Whichever way anyone comes to the moment of dying, it can be seen as the fulfilment of the living which has preceded it. Death may bring to an end what is; it can never devalue what has been. In the end dying is not the opposite of living, but rather the completion of it.

Caring for a loved one

Isobel McDonagh
Macmillan nurse, who nursed her husband until his death

'The prognosis is not good.'
Yet he lives now ...
Father ... Dad ...
You never think
You never consider
Until the reality of our mortality
Hits us hard and painfully.
The childish, innocent,
uncomplicated view
of all things continuing,
        eternally,
        forever,
        as they are
        so they will be
is shattered once and for all.
The thought cannot settle in my mind
It cannot find a place
        a niche
where it will be accepted.
It has entered but it is not welcome,
I forget it,
        I ignore it,
        but never am I unconscious of it.
It bumps and bruises
hurts and maims,
Yet I refuse to grant it settlement.
My eyes look only to life.
They meet with life as they find
    their way to Dad.

Death has not come
He is immortal for some time ....
    Yet!

This was written by my teenaged daughter on the evening she heard that her father was dying. She has, in her own way, expressed the overwhelming struggle to understand what is happening: the struggle between what is and what will be. This period is the most difficult for the family and friends of a dying person. What lies ahead is unknown and is so unacceptable. In the emotional distress the confidence and the competence which are normally present evaporate.

How can I cope? Will I cope?

Being afraid of the future can paralyse the present. Although the dying person is isolated in the despair of the moment, the presence of others who also care does help, and sharing the distress and helplessness creates a bond. Friends and family are intertwined and the sharing of feelings is so important especially where children are concerned. To be excluded for any reason can cause problems later. The youngest member of a family can be an important part of the network of loving support for the person who is dying. To acknowledge the truth is not to deny the possibility of a remission of the disease but to support each other in the present situation. To face facts head on, to understand implications and then to live a day at a time, is a daunting task. It is also the first step on the journey of bereavement, but this is only seen in retrospect.

Gradually disbelief gives way to clearer thinking. It is then that you discover you have not understood all that you were told. In fact you are uncertain if you heard aright. So ask for another opportunity to hear what you may not have understood in shock. Bring a friend or relative with you to talk to the doctor, to confirm your understanding, because medical jargon is confusing and raises many questions. You can write down the questions you wish to ask, those questions that have been tumbling round in your mind since the first interview. Your need is for explanations: of the expected progress of the disease, of treatment and medication, of available support and help, of the 'next step'. Even the questions you might think of as silly must be asked. If you are to give your loved one the very best care possible, you must

understand and trust the professionals around you. You must know who you can turn to for help.

Your greatest need at this time is for emotional support. Help is needed to separate the self-centred cry of despair and the other-centred cry of love. The marshalling of the inner resources you hardly knew were there creates the courage which is born of love. You are central for the patient and you will discover you can do things for your loved one you never thought possible. We all deny death: it happens to others. Because we too will die, we identify with the dying person. It will happen to us one day. Because of this we experience fear in the face of death. We are afraid of the responsibility, of failure in our care, afraid of the future, afraid of our own health. Fear loses its terror when we are able to speak about it, and to acknowledge the reality of this will help.

When friends tell us to 'be brave' or 'it will be OK' or 'cheer up', it adds to the distress and the loneliness of not being understood. No one knows exactly how you feel, for you are unique and your relationship with the dying person is also unlike any other. Those who have been through a similar experience may understand but cannot know your feelings. With this is mind it may help to seek out a person who will listen and understand. This person may be a nurse, a doctor, minister, priest or a close friend. Sometimes the Macmillan sister fulfils this counselling role.

Moving from the shock and distress of the first few days, you will find that you, as carer, need encouragement. In hospital or at home you have a key role. The confidence and calm which comes from planning care with the professionals involved can be yours because you know in a special way the wishes and needs of the patient. In the day-to-day care of your loved one, what you observe and report is essential for medical and nursing care.

Adapting to the practicalities of caring at home may be difficult, but they are easiest when the patient first comes home from hospital. You should choose the brightest, airiest room with a view, with easy access to bathroom, space for armchairs and a shelf, bed table or similar, with adequate room for books, drinks, tissues – the paraphernalia of illness. Mirrors sometimes cause problems with their constant reminder of loss of weight and changing body image. The double bed should not be replaced until necessary for nursing care. For couples the continuing intimacy of their relationship is part of the comfort each can give the other.

The day-to-day landscape for the family is of many hills and valleys. There will be days when you ask yourself 'Is it true?' or when you live

in a fantasy of 'They were wrong'. There are other days when misery, guilt or anger overwhelms you: guilt at being tired, of not caring enough or of having ignored or denied the early signs of illness. It is impossible to disentangle the suffering of the patient and the close relative. There is the split of knowing and feeling, of head and heart being on different tracks. Throughout this time there is often a lift of the heart, when all seems well, only for it to plummet again. The painful anticipation of the visit to the clinic includes the hope of good news... even now! With many lifts of spirit the anticipation becomes harder to bear. You rejoice for the patient but you weep inside.

Each day is so precious, yet the need now is for normality, the paradox of holding abnormality in a normal setting. Life for the children at school, the daily chores, the weekly routine, must go on as before – but not quite. The supermarket, workplace or school are full of continuous anxious requests for news. The phone becomes the tyrant of the repeated story of sadness. A friend, who took over the phone, made a list of callers, whom she held at bay with every one's gratitude for her thoughtfulness and understanding. There will be times of laughter and humour. My experiences as a nurse in a hospice gave me new insights into the human spirit. To celebrate life in the midst of death was a daily occurrence. Gentle celebration of birthdays, anniversaries, a new baby in the family, a wedding or even a good night were reasons enough.

There will be quiet times when words fail, and intimacy and touch express the sadness together. Shared memories of happy times and of family holidays may lead to the long-delayed sorting of photographs. There will be noisier times when visitors become a problem. You love to see them come because they care about you and yours, but do they not know when to leave? You watch for the weariness that exacerbates pain and causes sleeplessness. You feel like a guard dog, sometimes snarling beneath the polite smile at some people's thoughtlessness. A strategy is needed which can be worked out together if both of you are to enjoy the visits.

A note of caution – your need to protect, to spoil, to fuss may cause distress for others: distress for the patient whose independence is decreasing because of the illness and the little that is left is being taken away by you; distress for other close relatives whose need you are ignoring, like parents of the husband or wife. Those who love will grieve and grief is affected by what goes before. Allowing others to do what you want to do and could do better is difficult. I remember sitting on the bottom step of the stairs in tears as my son helped his dad to settle for the night. The chatter and

laughter only made it worse and it was only 48 hours before my husband's death. Watching you, the carer, the patient often senses your distress and can become anxious about your health and irritable out of frustration and helplessness. Admission to hospital is often at the request of the patient because he or she feels such a burden. Talking this through and asking for help can often change this. Your loved one is making a journey of grief, of losing everything. To acknowledge their sadness, anger or despair will help more than the cheery 'You'll be up and about in no time.' It takes courage to sit down, listen, to hold your loved one like a child and perhaps cry together. Confirming what the patient already knows or suspects will leave no room for playing games of deceit when what is needed is loving support. It is much easier than you would expect. Your sorrow will meet theirs and the truth sets free all the love you have for each other, putting aside the pretence which separates and isolates each in their own misery. This is a gift of parting, which although so sad can be very beautiful. I look back in wonder and amazement at this time.

As the illness progresses and the patient becomes weaker the landscape changes again. The hills are not so high, the valleys not so deep. The reality of death has become part of your life. Little by little you let go, but it is not easy. Anxieties about pain or discomfort from other symptoms preclude anxieties about the future. A calm and peaceful night is a cause for gratitude. It is my experience that, as death comes nearer, the patient gradually withdraws from the people around. This is seen even when no drugs are needed for symptom control. It is as if nature's way of letting go will match our letting go. To allow our loved ones to let go is the last gift we can give them. The nurses who share our care of the patient will gradually prepare the family for the physical signs of imminent death. To know what may happen and why it is so takes the fear out of a new experience. The availability of help if courage fails or loss overwhelms is essential to allow a family to cope in their own way. What must be done in practical ways should be planned ahead. When death comes, the quiet time to say goodbye need not be rushed and permission to take as long as is needed can be reassuring for the family. A list of phone calls to hand to a friend or relative, the choice of funeral director, what the dead should wear, the service, hymns – all are decisions which are more difficult to make in the time of immediate grief. Feelings can be hurt and people forgiven in the bewilderment of the finality of death. Regrets add to the sorrow.

The network of family and friends is made up of many individuals of all ages. Each will have had a different relationship with the dead person. Their grief is special and needs expression in their own way. This is so for the teenager, the elderly parent, the small child and the middle-aged aunt. Sharing within the family can be a time for growth and will affect their lives. Suppressed grief can be destructive. The care of a loved one will continue for those he or she loved as friends or family. As a nurse I have seen the 'heartbreak at the heart of things' and struggled often with the problem of suffering. I was taught that one of the needs of a dying patient was to find meaning in what was happening. My own search for meaning in what life is about has been immeasurably helped by my dying patients. Their courage and honesty has enriched my life. The loving care of families and friends who surround a dying person gives value and meaning to the importance of all our relationships as human beings. As a widow I look back to the eight months of caring for a dying husband as a very special time. I can see it now as a paradox of heartbreak and joy in the middle of the tumult of grief.

Love is not changed by Death
and nothing is lost and all in the end
is harvest.

Edith Sitwell

The face of death

The Rev. Peter Speck
Chaplain, Royal Free Hospital, Hampstead

Christine was 35 when she was first diagnosed as having a terminal illness. The news was devastating. She was married and had two young children, aged ten and seven years. She entered a very active treatment programme and responded well, so that during the next two years she lived her life to the full and had more time with her family. Sadly, her disease returned and she and her family had to face the fact that she was dying.

Christine's husband, Tom, had always had a fear of dying and so when he knew that her death was imminent he both wanted to be there and yet wished to be a million miles away. Tom had never seen anyone die, except on the TV, nor had he seen a dead body, so there was much that he imagined about the event. Staff explained and offered reassurance that the final part of a life (whatever has happened beforehand) is usually very peaceful. Christine also had much anxiety about dying, although death itself was not frightening for her. As time progressed Christine spent more time sleeping. When she woke up she would look around to see who was there and would ask for Tom and her family. If Tom was there she found it very comforting to have him sitting on or near to the bed so that they could touch and talk to each other quietly. The children (now twelve and nine) also visited Mum and opportunity was given for them to ask questions and talk about Mum dying with staff or family members.

One morning Christine's condition dramatically changed. She went into a very deep sleep and her breathing pattern changed. She was mainly breathing through her mouth and Tom and the staff moistened her lips and mouth regularly to prevent them becoming dry and sore. Her breathing became rattly because of the secretions in her throat and there would sometimes be long gaps between breaths. Tom and the family found this disconcerting, since just as they were beginning to think Christine had died, she would suddenly take a very deep breath. It was clear to all that Christine was quite peaceful and that there was no pain or agitation. The children were asked whether they wished to be at the bedside or remain with friends. They both wished to be with Dad and so the whole family was present when Christine eventually died. At the moment of death Tom noticed that Christine had taken 'one of her deep breaths' and he said that 'after a while there was a very faint whisper of breath and then all the muscles of her face seemed to relax and she looked so peaceful.' Instead of being the fearful event he had anticipated he later described it as 'painful but beautiful'. The nurse contacted the doctor who came to see Christine and to confirm that she had died.

At this point several members of the family found that they knew within their heads that Christine was dead but were unable within their hearts to believe it. It frequently takes time for this sort of knowledge to register properly even when one is present at the time of death. It is even more important, therefore, for people to be given every opportunity to visit and see the person who has died in order to acknowledge the reality of death, the need to 'let go', and to initiate the natural grieving process. The use of the word 'opportunity' is important since it is not a case of making people view someone who has died but ensuring that this opportunity is not denied to them. This is especially so with children. It is tempting to become overprotective of children and to assume that they are 'too young to know'.

Since many people, like Tom, have never seen a dead body it is helpful if an explanation can be given of what they are likely to see, before they go into the room, whether at home, hospital or a funeral director's chapel of rest. This is especially relevant following a traumatic death in an accident, or where there may be changes in the appearance of a person because of the nature of the death, like the colour of the skin.

In many ways the best time to see someone who has died is immediately after the death while the body is still reasonably warm and it is still in the bed – at home or in hospital. This certainly gives death a more natural feel for many people than going later to a funeral director's when the body has been transferred to a coffin. After a time the body cools and *rigor mortis* sets in. The skin takes on a waxy, translucent quality which some people feel highlights the fact that the person is dead, and can lead to comments such as 'It doesn't look like...' Chris or Jim or whomever. On the other hand, if someone has not been able to be present at the time of death, or soon afterwards, it can sometimes be more difficult to believe that the person has died, and therefore to see the body at that later time can be very helpful.

Not having a body to focus on and to grieve over can also create difficulties for people in initiating the natural process of grief. This will sometimes happen when the person has died in a fire, or an explosion, or a body has not been recovered for some other reason. It can be important and helpful if there is something to use as a focus and means of establishing the identity of the dead person, like a ring, or a piece of clothing. One woman following the death of her husband in a fire said: 'Going to identify his body terrified me. I dreaded what I was going to see. The police and the social worker were marvellous and explained that I would not see everything... When I went into the room his body was completely covered up in a green cover. I sat by it for a while and then touched his arm and felt his hand. The lady who was with me then uncovered his hand and I saw the signet ring I had given him a few years before. I knew it was him. It hurt so much, my chest hurt with sobbing, but I knew it was him. There was a vicar there who said some prayers. That helped... I don't remember much more.'

When people go to see someone who has died they may appreciate an opportunity to be alone with the dead person so that they can say some of the things they may feel too embarrassed to say in front of someone else. This can include feelings of love, guilt and shame as well as anger. After sitting by the body of her dead husband for an hour, Joan eventually stood up and screamed at him: 'What right have you to die and leave me with two teenage children to bring up on my own ... it's bloody typical of you!' and then stormed out of the room, and broke down and cried.

It is helpful not to rush people at this time since they *need time* in order to take in what has happened. Some family members appreciate an opportunity to share in the washing of the body after death, either as part of their religious and cultural practices (as in Judaism and Islam) or as a further expression of their loving care for the deceased before saying their final 'goodbye'. If we are not of the same religious or cultural background as the family of the deceased it is important to be flexible in how we respond to their needs. Some families will want to have a priest, minister or other religious person present to say appropriate prayers when they see the body. Others may wish to 'keen' or 'wail' at the bedside. What is important is that in some way people are enabled to say their 'goodbye' in the way that seems most appropriate to them.

Sensitivity is also called for in acknowledging the variety of relationships that may have existed between the dead person and those who are present at the time of death, or who come to see that person after death. In the case of divorce, a previous partner or the children of a previous marriage may wish to come. This can cause tensions within the present family and these can sometimes be eased in advance if the person who is dying is able to make some of their wishes and feelings known about whom they wish to see or not see. This can be difficult in hospital since ward staff can feel caught in a family dynamic and asked to take sides or prevent certain people from visiting. A similar situation can arise if the dying person has an extramarital relationship unknown to the spouse. Permission to grieve may be denied to some people since their relationship with the deceased may not be known and so not only may visiting be impossible prior to death, but viewing the body and attending the funeral also.

Couples in gay relationships will anticipate some of these problems by making a will containing an appropriate declaration about who is the 'significant other person' for them, which may not be the person usually deemed as their next of kin. Whilst this does not preclude tense scenes at the bedside of the dying person because, for example, of the anger of parents towards a gay partner, nevertheless the various organisations which exist within the gay community have done a great deal to help people be more open with their families about their relationships and their wishes in the event of serious illness.

The events leading up to a death may be distressing and alarming to the persons watching, and to the dying themselves in the case of violent death. However, the actual moment of death is always peaceful for the person who is dying and, in the case of those who have had 'near-death experiences', has been described sometimes as a relief. Following the death, permission needs to be given to people to express their grief in the way that is right for them, and being with the dying and seeing the body afterwards are very important factors in initiating natural grieving and a more healthy personal future.

The death of a child

Jillian Tallon, National Secretary of Compassionate Friends

'People commented that we could always have "another one" as if a lost child was a piece of broken china from a dinner service – easily replaceable!'

'All death is difficult to deal with and talk about, but the death of a child is probably the most difficult. The usual words of comfort given to the loved ones of an older person are totally useless and therefore the parents are usually met with silence.'

We were awoken by Anneli's screams. We had three sons under two years old, and Anneli was our helper. She had gone into the twins' room to begin the morning routine of changing and feeding Oliver and Timothy who were almost six months old. The doctor had called the evening before because we had all been unwell with colds and flu, had looked at the twins and said, 'Oliver's fine now, we don't need to worry about him, but old Tim's a bit chesty.' But next morning, New Year's Eve 1967, Oliver was dead. (At that time, 'cot death' was not given as a cause of death on the certificate, so it said 'bronchiolitis'.)

We were utterly devastated, shocked and bewildered. Yes, 'cot death' was known, but it was very rare and, classically, only happened to 'other people'. Not us, not our son. But Oliver was dead in my arms, even though I had tried to revive him. Our doctor was round in ten minutes, and the machinery of death moved into action. The coroner's officer (who was not in uniform) was very kind, and he gave us the name of a local funeral director. I'm sure the director did his best, but I will not forget the horror of seeing him leave our house with a large suitcase. It seemed then, and still does, a dreadful way to take a dead baby away.

'How did you cope?' For us, it was Tim and his elder brother of 20 months, Alastair, who kept us sane, functioning and loving. Neither had any conscious understanding of what had happened. There was no way we could explain to them that their brother had died, and they needed their breakfast straight away. So, in some ways, we had no time for realisation and adjustment. Alastair and Tim needed us and we simply had to get on with it. Both sets of grandparents lived nearby and came round immediately; my sister, whose own baby was only three months old, came from the other side of London, and a number of friends came too. But to the question 'How did you cope?' I have no real answer. I believe that many people, devastated and numbed by shock, somehow instinctively switch to 'automatic pilot'. We carry on functioning (and that includes crying, weeping, sobbing) but something internally protects us from fully experiencing all that we are feeling. That may sound a bit contradictory, but I do not think that in the early stages (perhaps as long as three months or so) we are able to comprehend the magnitude and the profundity of our loss.

If we are frank, we all think that our parents will die before us; our husband, wife, partner may die before us. But our child? Never! It is inconceivable that we will attend our daughter's or son's funeral. That is why the death of a child (even if that 'child' is well into middle age at the time of death) is so devastating.

If it does happen, we are utterly unprepared. How can we possibly prepare for something that seems so unnatural and against nature? It may be different for parents who have had to endure the agony of nursing a dying child over weeks, months or perhaps even years; nevertheless, when the death occurs, their feelings are little different from anyone else's. They may have been able to give some thought to the funeral, to the other children in the family, their responses, reactions, needs. There may have been time to say 'goodbye', but most experience the full range of emotional and physical reactions felt by others whose children die suddenly.

Shock, disbelief, bewilderment, fear, anger, resentment, despair, overwhelming grief and misery, anxiety, denial, agitation, bitterness, guilt are some of the emotions that overtake us. There is no pattern, no sequence, no 'norm'. There is chaos, confusion, turmoil, extreme swings of mood and activity. Some are immobilised, frozen, cut off from themselves and from those around them. Others seek endless busyness, cannot be still or alone, keep talking rapidly and repetitively. Some may be unable to think or do anything for themselves; others will bake like mad, dig up the garden, turn out cupboards. There may be variations from one extreme to another. All of this comes within the range of 'normal'.

'I thought I was well armed to deal with

it. I knew what to expect (or so I thought). In reality one's feelings are indescribable... It is as if one has been bodily transported to a strange world of which you know nothing.'

'Oh for someone to talk to – my friends admitted later that they had sat in their own homes and cried – we could have helped each other to cry together.'

Not only do we have to cope with our own feelings, but we also have to cope with other people's too. So many bereaved people feel isolated from others by the experience. Everyone feels that their situation is unique – and they are absolutely right. Each experience of bereavement *is* unique. A father and a mother will have had different relationships with their child, different experiences of her or him, different responses to her or him. So no one can say 'I know exactly how you feel,' even where there are striking outward similarities. 'I can imagine how you are feeling,' 'I know something of what you are feeling,' those may well be true. But no one really knows.

This means that each one of us has to find our own way along the painful road of bereavement. It is rough, it is uneven, it is discouraging, at times we fall in a heap at the wayside, we may even go a little way back, but ultimately one day the pain will begin to ease.

Who can help us? Our own family,

to begin with. We all need each other, and in helping our partner or child we are at the same time helping ourselves. Each time we turn to someone else and hold out our hand to help them, we too are strengthened by that contact, and by the experience of helping someone else. It may be no more than crying together, holding each other, mopping up each other's tears. But that very togetherness will help to diminish the sense of isolation that so many bereaved people feel. This can be just as true for children as for adults. Many of them feel terribly isolated from their friends when they are struggling with bereavement, so they need opportunities at home to talk about what is going on inside them.

'Graham was four when James died. Quite old enough to understand why his brother wasn't moving. He was not excluded and all the endless questions were answered. It's not easy to do this, but in the long term it's much better.'

But other family members suffer too, particularly grandparents. Whilst trying to be strong for their 'child' who is bereaved, they are, of course, grieving for the loss of their grandchild as well. Also, irrationally but understandably, grandparents may feel that it is they who should have died, that they have lived a long and useful life whereas their grandchild has had only a short life.

Parents who have lost a child may be too devastated and shocked to consider and care for their other children. It is to be hoped that there will be other relatives or family friends who can help look after the children, not necessarily by taking them away from home, but by calling frequently, perhaps being there when the children come home from school, taking them out at weekends, whatever is appropriate to the number and ages of the children. It may be helpful for someone other than the parents to contact the nursery or playgroup, school(s), out-of-school activities (swimming, dancing, Cubs, Guides, etc.), employer, workmates, the GP, the local minister (where appropriate), the funeral director. But it is best to discuss this with the parents and see how much of this sort of help they want; some may feel their role is being usurped, or that they are being 'taken over'. 'Would you like me to let the school know what has happened, or would you prefer to speak to them yourself?' The parent is likely to give a specific response which will enable the helper to respond appropriately, leaving the parent neither neglected nor overburdened.

What else helps us to cope? Talking to others who have experienced much of what we are going through. Family and friends may find it very difficult to talk, or to allow us to talk, of the child who died, but others who have had a similar experience can provide a place and space for you to talk of him or her; they will feel for you, and they will support you, but they will not be as directly affected as your child's grandparents, aunt or uncle, close friends, all of whom may have known the child well. There are organisations which exist for the purpose of sharing these experiences and support, and these are listed at the end of the book. They are befriending organisations, which means that members of each of them have experienced that particular kind of death, and so are most able to help, to support, to encourage, to share.

People who have not been bereaved are often reluctant or afraid to speak of the child who has died. But the bereaved person has not forgotten for one second the one they have loved and lost. It is in the forefront of their mind and heart the whole time and, when the loved one is seemingly ignored, the hurt is intense. Most people, especially when they are newly bereaved, are looking for opportunities to talk of their child and are fearful that the child's existence and life will be forgotten or obliterated. So the non-bereaved need to be brave, to risk tears and talk, and to mention the child by name as naturally as possible. The more opportunities a bereaved parent is given to talk of their child (or children), the less frantically they will seek for the opportunities that are denied them.

'It as though, to some people, my daughter never existed and this is one of the most hurtful and thoughtless things people can do.'

'If only people could realise that if they mention my daughter I will not burst into tears but will appreciate that they haven't forgotten her and that this will give me great comfort.'

Why this need to talk of the dead child?

We do not stop loving someone simply because they are not physically present. If people go on holiday or emigrate, we go on loving them; we do not stop simply because they are not near us.

Equally, love does not cease with the issuing of a death certificate; it is not a tap to be turned on and off. Love fires us, love inspires us, love is the natural impulse of a parent for their child. Their love for us remains with us; our love for them continues to the end of our days, no matter how short or long a time we knew our child.

'I will never get over losing my son, nor do I want to. I have been told by another bereaved parent that you don't get over it, you just, in time, cope better with it.'

'As with all major events in life, death changes people – accepting our baby's death means that we can talk freely and with joy about him, although sadness still wells up in all of us from time to time.'

The contact address for Compassionate Friends, and several other organisations dealing with particular forms of child death (miscarriage, stillbirth, cot death) are listed at the end of the book.

The funeral

Christopher and Sandra Wickenden, undertakers

'Will you be requiring burial or cremation?' At a time of deepest distress, the starkness of that question can feel incredibly wounding, but shortly after the death of a friend or relative, the undertaker will need to know which method you have chosen.

A decision is required at a time when the whole world seems in chaos and any decision, however small, seems mountainous. As you work through your grief, the way that the funeral is conducted can make a considerable difference in the long term. It may not feel like it now but you can come through this experience, and this particularly difficult time can help you in your subsequent journey through grief. Included here are some ideas on how best to cope if you find yourself having to arrange a funeral or helping someone who has this task to face. Some of these ideas may not feel right for you; it may be that your religion demands a very rigid structure. That is fine, but if you think that there might be room for something else or just are not aware of what options are available, then take any of these ideas and make them work for you.

Where to start

The best place to start is before a death actually takes place. If, whilst in good health or even during illness, we make our own final arrangements, this can relieve the people left behind of a real burden. We are carrying out the funeral this week of a lady who 'prearranged' her funeral with us. Three months ago Mrs Smith was told that she had only a short time to live. She came into our offices with her daughter and made all the arrangements for her own funeral. Last week her husband came in and told us that she had died in one of the local hospitals. He told us that his wife had found it a great relief to know that everything had been taken care of with people she trusted and that her last wishes would be respected; this helped him cope too.

However, as the roadside walker replied to the traveller who asked the way to Dorking, 'Well mate, if I were you, I wouldn't start from here!' So if you find yourself having to make all the decisions without the deceased leaving any guidelines, what should you do?

To view or not to view

'Viewing' is the term undertakers use when people want to see the person who has died before the funeral. This can be at home or at the chapel of rest. If you decide to see the deceased you may like to arrange for him or her to be dressed in their own clothes. Do make sure that you tell the undertaker whether or not you require make-up to be applied, as it can be quite upsetting if you are not expecting to see it. Make sure that the chapel of rest is nice. Some undertakers have much brighter and more tasteful chapels than others, so ask to see the chapels if you would like to be reassured that they are suitable. Whilst you are doing that, also check whether or not there is an additional charge for the use of the undertaker's chapels.

What do I do there?

Once you are with the deceased in the chapel, you may like just to look and remember some of the times you spent together. Some people say a prayer, others will talk to the deceased. Use the time as you want. If you want to touch the person, then do. You could put some mementoes in the coffin, like a photograph, lucky charm, letters or even a favourite book of the deceased. Rosary beads are often placed around the hands of Catholics.

Some people like to go as a family, and in some Asian religions, the preparation of the body by the relatives is very important. If that is the case for you, make sure that the undertaker has adequate facilities and is understanding about your needs before you commit yourself to using a particular company.

Burial or cremation?

Burial

The decision you make will depend a lot on your culture and traditions. Burials can take place in an existing family grave or a new grave. Burials tend to be more expensive than cremations. Traditionally a solid wood rather than veneered coffin is used, but a veneered coffin is quite sufficient if that is what you prefer. Some folk feel that a grave has a feeling of permanence about it and it does give those grieving a specific place to visit in the days or years after the funeral. It also means that in due course you can erect a memorial on the site; but do remember that memorials can be very expensive. However, if there are financial restrictions at present it may be that you would appreciate having the option to buy a memorial at a later date when circumstances allow.

You can have the funeral service at a church, place of worship, undertaker's chapel, cemetery chapel or at the graveside. Graveside services can be very moving, but in our unpredictable climate it does well to remember that bad weather can distract from the service. Some cemetery chapels are lovely, but others may not be well heated and have little or no facilities for music. You could have the service at the place of your choice and then have a short 'committal service' at the graveside (committal for a burial being the act of placing the coffin in the ground). Choose what best serves your particular circumstances.

Cremation

Most people seem to prefer cremation to burial at the present time. Cremation can be cheaper than burial and a veneered coffin is usually used. You can use the crematorium chapels for the whole service or just the committal. Crematoria have different arrangements for the process of the committal: some have small doors that open and the coffin leaves the mourners by being pulled through the doors; others have curtains that close in front of the coffin. You may like to leave the coffin on the catafalque at the front of the crematorium chapel at the end of the service and then leave the chapel. Some people feel that this gives a feeling of unfinished business and prefer to say their final goodbyes as the coffin leaves them.

A record is always kept of where ashes are scattered in the crematorium gardens, although there is not a specific grave. These gardens are often beautifully kept, providing a lovely setting to return to, perhaps for an anniversary or birthday of the deceased. There may be books of remembrance opened each day at the appropriate page. Brass plaques and other memorials may also be offered. You may prefer to take the ashes away from the crematorium and have them placed in the family grave. Alternatively, as is becoming increasingly popular, a cemetery will provide small cremated remains plots which allow for a bronze plaque or other small memorial to be placed on the site.

Most crematoria have one or two chapels which tend to be bright and warm with facilities for live or taped music. However, they can become very busy and to avoid the possibility of 'bumping into' other mourners it may be worthwhile reserving a chapel for two sessions. This will cost more but you may consider the privacy worth it.

A word of advice on the matter of cost. It is understandable to want the best for the departed, but beware the temptation to spend more than you can afford. Bereavement can make one vulnerable and the amount of money that you spend on a coffin is not indicative of the amount of love you feel for someone. If you are in any doubt about the quality of a coffin, ask to see an example. You can also ask for a price list and you should receive an estimate for the funeral before the funeral day arrives.

Why is the funeral service important?

Often the first response to a bereavement is one of shock and disbelief: 'I can't believe it's true.' The funeral service can help to make the facts of the death real. This can be painful but is necessary for grieving to proceed unhindered. Although for most people there is no longer a fixed period of mourning the existence of an accepted fixed procedure and ritual gives a sense of security in the chaos of bereavement. Funerals can serve to rally sympathy from the family, giving people an opportunity to talk about the deceased, share stories and express their sorrow and support. Realistically, although it is true that family differences can be forgotten at a time such as this, a death in the family can also heighten tensions and old conflicts may return. If that happens, support from friends and neighbours, emotional or practical, can be particularly helpful. Funerals will also help people to begin to accept the change in status that a death

may bring, perhaps from being married to being single again as a widow or widower.

The service itself

A few simple additions will make the funeral service a much more meaningful event. By the time the funeral day arrives a real relationship should have been built up between the family and the undertaker. In that way, when the funeral cortège arrives at home, and the undertaker knocks on the door, it is more like greeting a trusted friend than being introduced to a complete stranger.

In some religions the funeral service is of greater significance for the person who has died than for the mourners, but whether or not a minister or priest takes part, it is also a public act showing concern for the bereaved and/or respect for the departed. Christopher conducted a funeral recently where there was hardly anyone present who actually knew the person who had died; however, the chapel was quite full. Those present were mostly friends of the deceased's daughters who wanted to show their support and love for their friends at a time of crisis. The daughters were very touched by their presence and it helped greatly at a very difficult time.

If you do not know a minister or priest, then talk to relatives and friends or ask your undertaker for guidance. As with all professions, some people are gifted in particular areas and this may include taking a funeral service. Some ministers are good at taking funerals, some are not.

For most people it is helpful to have someone leading the service and it is important that this person takes time to find out about the person who has died. I well remember one service which I attended. Everything was acceptable except for one important thing. The minister taking the service insisted on calling the deceased Percy. That was the name on the death certificate but to friends and family alike he had always been known as Bob. The discomfiture of the mourners, myself included, became more and more noticeable as he used the name Percy again and again. It was a great relief when it was all over.

As a general rule, the more you can be involved in the arranging of the funeral service the more meaningful it can become for you. Thus it can become more helpful in terms of grieving and loss. This does not necessarily mean having overall responsibility for the service; that depends on the individual. It may well be better to have someone who is not so emotionally involved actually taking the service. Very often the minister or priest will be happy to build personal elements into the overall structure of the service.

Whoever you ask to lead the service must feel comfortable in the role. Groups of musicians or singers may be used, and most undertakers will tell the story of the occasional jazz band. Favourite hymns and live or taped music may be used on entrance or exit from the church or crematorium. Favourite readings from the Bible, poems, extracts from letters or prose may also be read out. One often welcome addition is a tribute or address from the front about the deceased person. Personal recollections, a brief history about the deceased and extracts of letters sent to the family about him or her can be pulled together in the form of a tribute. However it is important for the content to be based realistically on the character of the deceased, since everyone has less positive sides to their natures.

Beliefs about life and death can be shared, and religious leaders often supply support, not only spiritually but also in other real and practical ways in the ensuing days. Do not reject the established church out of hand as you will find a degree of expertise seldom to be found elsewhere.

In thinking about ways of making the service special, one particular funeral springs to mind. A lady had died and left instructions in her will about how we were to carry out her funeral. Her husband Bill had died some years earlier and was, shall we say, of a rather colourful character, often returning very late from his 'recreation'. As she was lowered into the grave to be laid at rest with her husband, the churchyard was filled with the sound of a single saxophonist playing 'Won't you come home, Bill Bailey, won't you come home?' There were a few wry smiles as well as tears that day.

The day of the funeral will be one that you will want to remember and look back on, if not at that time, then later on. With this in mind, it may be an idea to have someone take photographs of those attend ing the service or of the flowers sent on the day of the funeral. Some people take photos of the coffin itself as a reminder.

As the pain of the first days of bereavement dulls, you will be able to remember with a sense of satisfaction the funeral in which you had taken a part in arranging. Be encouraged that one day you will remember the day with a smile as being a sad but important event in your life: a fitting farewell for somebody special which played a not insignificant part in moving you through the grief journey.

Letting the grief out

by Dr Grant Blair, London GP

There are few things in life ascertain as our own death and those of the ones we love. This universal experience, which for many is the most challenging of their lives, is seldom talked about and poorly understood. At its worst it leaves people with emotions they do not understand and with no one to talk to.

Whilst everyone's experience varies, bereavement does follow a general pattern. Initially with the news of the death comes shock and disbelief, as if the enormity of what has happened cannot be taken on board. This is often followed by a variety of emotions that come and go in a confusing fashion: tears, emotional outbursts, guilt and frustration. Anger too may be felt and this may be directed at the person who has died ('How dare he leave me like this?'). These dreadfully acute emotions tend in time to be replaced by depression and gloom. Slowly, with support, there comes an acceptance and some sort of readjustment.

As well as the psychological there are the physical symptoms of grief which are sometimes not recognised for what they are. They may include palpitations, chest pain, poor sleep, loss of appetite or tiredness and may often lead to repeated visits to the doctor before the penny drops. 'Heartache' may frighten both the bereaved and the doctor.

This whole process can take up to two years, so it is important to give yourself time. Very often I find that people need reassurance that the pain will be less intense and that there is light at the end of the tunnel. On the practical side, it is best to try to postpone major decisions for six months or so, or until the grief has settled. Tempting though it may be to sell your house and move, these decisions taken in grief can be regretted at a later date.

How we cope with a loss can depend on many things, some of which may be beyond our control. The nature of the death is obviously important. The more expected, generally the easier the readjustment. Clearly the sudden death of a young child from a road traffic accident is much harder to bear than the gradual peaceful death of an aged grandparent. The suicide of a loved one is much more distressing than the expected death of a friend from a slow illness. Society, too, has ideas on what forms of death are 'acceptable'. Imagine the distress of having a partner die from AIDS and not feeling able to talk about it for fear of perhaps offending people. It is also true for other medical problems, for example alcoholism, drug addiction or mental illness. The difficulties the carers faced in life do not disappear in death.

Our own understanding of death also affects our response to it. Where do we feel our loved ones are? Will we meet them again? For some these questions are answered by faith, which can offer great solace. For others they are unanswerable, adding to the confusion and pain. For everyone there is a 'first' bereavement and this will often be the first time we have thought at any length about what death means.

The death itself may be an uncomfortable reminder of our own mortality, bringing with it a re-evaluation of our own lives in an attempt to focus on what is important. The implications for our work or personal lives are an additional stress at a difficult time.

I am often asked how I can bear being a doctor having to face death and disease every day. Don't I get depressed seeing people cope with serious illness? My answer is always the same, that whilst indeed I do come close to many painful experiences, I am often uplifted by the courage and strength that most people show in difficult times. I see far more bravery day by day than disaster.

Most people do cope. However, some people get stuck in their grief and a very small number may be overwhelmed by it. This can happen for several reasons. Grief is an active process that needs to be worked through, and for some the immediate cost in terms of pain is too high. They fear that if they really connect with their grief, and start to express it, they will lose control. Some fear the grief will cause a mental breakdown or major depression. Others are terrified of breaking down in public or of being unable to do anything other than cry. So they tend to 'block' the grief in some way. This may mean becoming very busy with something else, for example losing themselves in their work, or changing the subject if the dead person is mentioned – anything to stop themselves thinking about what has happened. These tactics may indeed be successful for a time, but eventually the stress begins to tell.

The grief demands attention and will not go until it is dealt with.

I am reminded of a patient who tragically had a series of losses in her life. She was happily married with a young son when her husband, then in his early thirties, died suddenly of a heart attack in her arms. A year later her son was diagnosed as having a rare brain disorder. She was warned that it would first lead to his paralysis and then his death. She nursed him lovingly for four years, watching him slip away. With his death at four in the morning went her will to live. This series of losses left her punch-drunk. She feared she would kill herself. The only way she felt able to cope was to not think about what had happened. Rejecting offers of counselling from a wide variety of agencies, she withdrew into her home and appeared to show no emotion. It has been some time since she lost her son and she is only now beginning to emerge from this prolonged period of denial. I asked her once, 'Do you think about your son often?' 'All the time,' she replied immediately, 'and not at all. If I let myself think of him once I'll never think of anything else.' Maintaining this 'emotional neutral' took every ounce of her energy, day in and day out, and nothing was left for living.

Some people get stuck in their grief by being unable to let go. This may hinge on 'unresolved business' with the deceased. People often express the wish to have just five minutes to talk to the dead person, 'If only I could have said this' or 'If only I had done that' being the two comments most often made. They need to be reassured that these feelings are inevitable. Sometimes one can role-play such a meeting, encouraging the person to address the deceased directly. This can be very helpful, letting out lots of pent-up emotion. In reality, this is an extension of what very often happens at home anyway. When you get to know people well enough, they will often admit to talking aloud to their dead partners when at home alone. This confession is usually made with an anxious expression, as if expecting the doctor to rush them to a psychiatrist. Again reassurance is needed. This is a normal way to grieve. It is very hard to suddenly have your partner removed from you. The house may be quiet and lonely; your friends may be avoiding you, being anxious not to disturb you in your grief. You may not have the society of work if retired and may go long periods without a proper conversation with anyone. What then could be more natural than a quiet chat to your loved one? The feeling of wanting to keep the deceased near and fresh in your mind may extend to other harmless domestic rituals: laying an extra place at the dinner table or perhaps preparing a special meal that he or she may have enjoyed. Hearing the voice of the deceased at home is also a common experience and people need to be reassured that this too is normal and will pass in time.

The grieving process may get stuck in other ways. Fairly early on following a death, those close to the deceased tend to start 'idealising' the dead person. It is not unusual to hear 'He was a perfect father and husband' or 'We were married for fifty years with never a cross word.' Society too dictates that one must not speak ill of the dead. Usually this idealisation is in time replaced with a more realistic understanding of the deceased's good and bad points. After all it does not undermine the strength of your love or affection for you to admit that occasionally they were stubborn or bad-tempered. Sometimes, however, people get stuck with the image of a perfect partner snatched away by death.

I am reminded of a lady who is now in her late seventies. She was married for almost forty years when her husband died suddenly of a stroke. It was no secret to me that their marriage, as well as its good points, was also at times very difficult. He had a short temper and was not slow at expressing his displeasure both verbally and physically. She found this very hard to accept when he was alive, being both depressed and ashamed by her situation. In some ways I felt his death might release her from a none too happy relationship. Sadly this was not the case. She could not admit to herself, after his death, that he had a bad side. Gradually as the months went by, he became ever more perfect in her memory, and all unhappiness was banished. Her inability to admit the serious flaws in his personality meant that she was unable to deal properly with his death. She became fixated on this saintly husband and spent a good part of each weekend at his grave. It was only when she felt able to talk about his bad side that she started to improve. With this came a lot of sadness, both at the failure of some aspects of their marriage and guilt about her inability to change him for the better. But with this adjustment came a genuine sadness at the loss of this complicated man whom she loved, warts and all. It was only after being honest with herself that she could start to let go.

Beware also of putting on a brave face too often. This may manifest itself in many ways: not wanting to cry when friends comfort you; holding back tears at the funeral so you do not upset your family; not talking about the death for fear of worrying people. We all do it to a certain extent, because we understand that life needs to go on, despite the dreadful pain we feel. However, we sometimes put on our brave faces too much. I remember a father and son who both had to cope with the sudden and unexpected loss of their wife and mother. This was complicated by the fact that she had died whilst away for the weekend visiting her brother. In many ways her death seemed unreal to them both. To compound the misery the real communicator in the family had been the dead woman. Father and son had no real tradition of talking together, let alone about anything as bewildering as death. Both very much wanted to be strong for each other but also to talk about their common loss. They did not know how to start and were anxious that they would upset each other if they did. With painful irony both were worried about each other's apparent inability to grieve. Sometimes being too brave means that you do not get the help you need and deserve.

Is there then an ideal death and bereavement? To a certain extent the bereavement depends on the circumstances of the death. The best deaths I have been involved with are those where both the family and the person dying are fully aware of what is happening. Whilst this can be harder initially for both parties, there is no doubt that this 'pre-bereavement' period before death can allow family business to be settled, papers put in order and goodbyes said. Nature is often very kind in these circumstances, allowing, for example, a family to have one last Christmas together before death. It also gives the doctor time to prepare the family for what is to come and a way to help them with their grief. It is noticeable how the relationship between a doctor and a family alters following such a death. It often becomes much closer and more intimate. This enhanced relationship also helps with the grief that follows.

I am sure there are no 'rules' for bereavement, but perhaps there are a few guidelines.

1. Most people manage with time.

2. Grief is better dealt with than not.

3. Most people who are bereaved need to talk, but are not always sure how to, or to whom.

4. Friends, families and neighbours should not feel they have to keep a distance. A sympathetic ear may make all the difference. No special training is needed.

5. If you feel despair, tell someone – perhaps your GP, a friend or a bereavement counsellor.

Finally, it is perhaps only after some time that you will be able to look back and realise that the grief and pain is the price you pay for loving somebody.

Helping the bereaved

Pamela Bemment

These guidelines were first drawn up five years ago, based on my own experience. They have since been recommended by many people involved in helping the bereaved.

Comfort: to soothe in grief, to console, to make comfortable. It sounds simple enough, but for thousands of kind, caring people it means embarrassment, real distress or even tears. Here are a few do's and don'ts for all those who say 'I just don't know what to say to you,' who long to help their forlorn friends, but just do not know how to start, and who are terrified of getting it wrong.

If you can manage it, and it is virtually impossible, try not to say 'How are you?' It is the most instinctive and well-intentioned remark. Everyone says it and unfortunately the bereaved usually feels obliged to say 'Fine, fine,' when they really mean 'I can't believe it' or 'OK,' when they really mean 'I can't bear it.' Perhaps instead you could ask gently 'How are you today?' acknowledging without putting it into words that there are good days and bad days and days that are just impossible. My greatest comfort came from those who just put their arms around me and hugged me, saying very little.

Do make telephone calls for a quick chat('How are things going with you today?') or to invite them round for a tea, coffee or a meal, even those you do not know very well. But, and this is very important, **don't** be hurt if they do not immediately take up your offer. There were many people in my village who just said, 'Don't be alone.' I did not ring very often or pop in but the knowledge that they were there for me was sustaining and I shall never forget their thoughtfulness. One very slight acquaintance used to phone me now and again at 4 pm or 7.30 pm because they were *her* low times of day and she thought they might also be mine. She told me to ring her at any time if I was blue because she never slept before 3 am. We had several midnight calls.

Do remember that because you may have found your bereaved friend out or occupied on the day you choose to call, it does not mean that they will be out or occupied every time you do so. I was told, 'You're never there,' but I was there for days on end on my own and then saw several people in one day. It is quite a good idea to make a quick phone call before you set out to say that you are on your way and you will be able to tell immediately whether it is a good idea or not. Curiously, at my lowest ebb, I did not make many calls myself for fear of spoiling another's day with my sadness and this was in spite of being told to do just that. Kindness abounds.

Do remember that the bereaved need to eat. They might have no appetite, they certainly will not want to think about eating. So, in the earliest days, do make sure there is food in the house for them. In those few days, do ask bereaved people if they would like you to accompany them on visits to undertakers, registrars, banks, solicitors. The face of necessary bureaucracy can feel very cold and confusing to the newly bereaved. It is so good to have a familiar face beside you.

I never experienced the desolation of knowing that someone had crossed the road rather than speak to me, but perhaps the following

tips may help those who panic at the sight of a bereaved person.

Do remember that very few people hate to be touched. A hand held even briefly when meeting or a quick hug can bring an enormous amount of warmth without words. You cannot really go about hugging comparative strangers, I suppose, but a hand laid gently on the arm and the words 'I'm so sorry to hear your news' or 'I've been thinking of you so much' are positive statements which need no reply but a returned pressure of hands and a 'thank you', which is about all that can be managed at first without tears.

It is perhaps wiser not to say 'Let me know if I can be of help in any way' unless you really do mean it. You may find yourself in a bit of a fix if taken at your word when you were just trying to find something to say, and there is, of course, always the fear that you will be 'taken advantage of'. Who wants to offer to cut the lawn a couple of times and then be expected to do it ever afterwards or find that the weekly shop always includes a long list from your neighbour? There has to be a balance here about what is really necessary, and it is also up to the bereaved to play their part so that when they ask for help their friend or neighbour knows it is really needed and appreciated.

Do talk about the dear departed. One of the most hurtful experiences for me was when people avoided mentioning my husband's name as if he had never existed. The reason for their silence, of course, was that they did not want to distress me, but I yearned to hear his name on another's lips. It was strange that some close friends were the ones mistakenly tactful about this whereas others, and many friendly acquaintances, had no problem with it at all. At a dinner table where an argument had reached an impasse, one of the participants turned to me and said fiercely, 'Lawrie would have agreed with me, wouldn't he?' I told her he most certainly would have – it was so natural and such a joy to have him brought back, if only for a few seconds. On another occasion, a neighbour of my mother, who lives by the sea, asked me how I was getting on on my own. I was very moved when she added, 'I'll never forget him ambling along with his camera bag over his shoulder. He was always so happy here.' It is just as important to try not to be embarrassed by the mention of the departed's name by the bereaved for 'To live in the hearts of those we love is not to die' and this means allowing the bereaved to talk about their loved one with or without tears, recalling past happiness, arguments or laughter. **Do** bear with them if they repeat themselves for a while because, in truth, they really cannot remember from day to day what they have said or who they have said it to.

Do tell someone who has been alone for some time that you still think of them. You would be surprised by how much warmth comes from this, especially when months have passed. It is very comforting to know that someone really means what they say and wishes you peace of mind.

However, if you wish to be a true comforter, please do not tell the recently bereaved how lucky they are, for if there is one thing they do not feel it is *lucky*. They know they are lucky to have their children, parents or home; lucky to have no money worries, their health, to have a good marriage. Lucky to have friends, to be alive, to have a pension. But they really do not want to be told that right away. Trying to come to terms with a great emptiness, they can generally do without well-intentioned exhortations to 'look on the bright side'. So try not to say a few days after the funeral, 'How lucky you are to have had him,' for if you can see that the relationship was good then the loss is tremendous, the wound deep and it is *too soon* to feel that way. Curiously, if you do not point out the silver linings it enables the bereaved, in time, to find them for themselves and to be able to say 'How lucky I've been.'

It can be just as hurtful to make comparisons. In my experience it has never helped me to bear pain when I am told that there are others worse off than myself. Of course there are, and probably they are much braver, but I have never understood why their suffering should make me feel better. Within days of my husband's death I had been told that I was much better off than two widows of my acquaintance whose husbands had died many years previously. I knew how fortunate I was to have two devoted children, a fond mother and true friends, and certainly I was much more fortunate than anyone on their own, but that did not lessen my grief. When someone dear to you dies, only you know how much this means to you and comparisons can only wound.

On a similar note, if there is anything seemingly calculated to depress the bereaved it is being 'jollied'. 'Never mind,' said some well-meaning friends, 'you'll feel better when the baby comes' At the time it seemed a curious exchange, the warmth of a husband and lover for that of a baby, my first grand-child. 'Never mind!' said the same people when five months after the baby's birth he and his parents had to go and live in the Far East for three years, 'you'll be able to look forward to the photos, letters and visiting them.' On the other hand, when someone said, 'Oh no! what will you do now?' I was able to reply, 'It isn't the end – I can visit them, thank goodness' and then talk about the wonderful new job that caused the move. 'Oh no! just when the baby has arrived,' allowed me to say,

'I just can't believe it – thank goodness it's only for three years.' Of course they were right in the end. The little baby sleeping on my breast did bring renewed strength and warmth, something to be cherished, but their timing had been just a bit wrong. So, **don** 't be jolly at first because, strangely enough, when you are not, it allows the bereaved to find a bit of backbone.

I feel that the words 'should', 'ought' and 'must' are best avoided.

'You ought to sell this house as soon as possible. It's too big for you now.'

'You must make a fresh start.'

'You ought to stay where your friends are.'

'You should/ought/must get a dog/cat/lodger to keep you company.'

So much advice. Perhaps it is kinder to question gently, 'Do you feel you want to stay here for a while?' or 'How do you feel about leaving here?' Be sure that whatever decision is made it will be over-turned just as quickly for if there is one thing very few bereaved people can do at this time it is make decisions. Some are acted upon immediately only to be regretted later, but there are others who make clean breaks and never look backwards. There is no set pattern. 'Float, mama,' said my daughter, 'life will take you over.' And I have been floating ever since, perfectly convinced that the first big decision I will make will be the wrong one, and this in spite of being a hopeful optimist.

Never say of anyone that they 'ought to have got over it by now'. Who sets time limits on grief or compassion? How can a person who has lived with someone for as many as fifty years or a parent grieving over a child recover their spirits to order? Six months, a year, two years on ... still be ready to ask how the bereaved is doing, and listen.

A final few words of hope for those who are alone, for what is life without sharing? It means making yourself go out and trying to return home in a positive frame of mind to a silent house. It means doing your best to plan optimistically for the years ahead. Nothing will be the same again. This has to be accepted finally, and with the help of friends and family, so generous with their love and caring, there will be happy times to help you bear this.

Facing the future

Pamela Winfield, author of book on widowhood

This chapter includes advice by some of the many people who wrote in response to the initial publicity around the series.

'Don't expect non-bereaved friends to think of inviting you on picnics, etc. They'll tell you about it, but it won't occur to them that you might like to have gone with them. My older daughter said at one of my low points, "Mummy, you've been through it and come out the other side. Their time is still to come, and then they will understand." '

'I would say that I am a stronger person now. Life is too precious to sit and mope about, but it's taken me nearly four years to come to terms with everything. People should realise when they say, "Oh, you should be over it by now," that it's not that easy.'

Facing the future after being bereaved is a process which has many ups and downs. The days can seem never-ending and the future seems bleak. But eventually you will come out the other side, even though bereavement is probably the greatest stress that any of us is likely to encounter. Whether the death is that of a parent, a partner, a child, there is a major adjustment to be made. An important relationship for us has come to an abrupt end and it takes time for us to learn to live with that. With the death of a spouse or partner, suddenly we are single again and discover that everyone else appears to be part of a couple. With the death of a parent, no matter our age, comes a feeling of being abandoned; and with the death of a child comes the shattering of hopes and dreams for the future.

Part of facing the future is to adapt to that change, but do not always expect other people to help you.

'I became a widower at the age of 37. One of my problems is friends' thinly concealed anxiety if they see me chatting to their wives – even if I've known them for years.'

'Other parents avoid me as I am a reminder to them that their children could also die.'

As a bereaved person you make the journey to acceptance on your own.

But are there any better ways of making that journey than others? What follows is based on my own experience and that of many widows I have spoken to, but much of this experience is applicable to other relationships as well.

The most important thing is to recognise who you are. Force yourself to stand in front of the mirror. The woman who stares back is a different you. You may not like her very much, but she is here to stay. 'You have to accept you are no longer somebody's wife.'

No one is suggesting that the grief will disappear with the touch of some magical wand. As someone told Lauren Bacall, 'Just know mmmthat every day, it gets the mtiniest bit better– suddenly one day you can put it into a different perspective.' The worst part is at the beginning when you feel the terrible sense of loss, so out of step with friends and glaringly aware how many people come in pairs, mmm but 'Don't think that because your husband has died this is the end of your life.' A new chapter is about to begin and you are in charge of writing it.

Time can be your greatest friend. Let some of it pass before you start making any irrevocable decisions such as moving home or throwing out all visible reminders of the person who has died. If you cannot bear to look at his or her clothes hanging in the wardrobe, close it tightly or move to another room for a while. In the days ahead there may well be favourite pieces of clothing which will be a great comfort. It was Daphne du Maurier who wrote in *Rebecca's Notebook and Other Memories* of her own widowhood. 'To ease the pain, I took over some of his things, wore his shirts, sat at this writing desk, used his pens to acknowledge the hundreds of letters of condolence and, by the very process of identification with the objects he touched, felt closer to him.'

The same applies to your home. Unless finance is desperate, sit tight. The first year is enough of an obstacle course of anniversaries, special events, and too many thoughts of 'if only' to add to it regrets for a hasty move.

A man who worked as a probate legal executive dealing with the estates of deceased clients, and who met many grieving relatives, offers the following advice:

'Always assuming reasonable fitness, my experience was that it was nearly always better for the widow/widower to return to the former matrimonial home

immediately after the funeral. Well-meaning relatives very often say, "Come back with us and stay as long as you like, Mother/Father!" This is seldom the best course of action. The bereaved has to come back to an empty house sometime and no one pretends that that is other than extremely difficult, but it is far, far more difficult to do so after being away from a shut-up house for several weeks. The emptiness has to be faced and is part of the readjustment following the death of one's partner – delaying this only makes matters worse. After a month, or maybe two, of starting to get used to the empty house, then go away for a short time if the offer is still open.'

'Another thing that often happens is that the matrimonial home is sold as quickly as possible after the death and mother/father goes to live with relatives. I could recount numerous instances where this has been done and then 18 months or so afterwards the widow has said to me, "I do wish I had stuck it out and stayed put. I really did not know what I was doing. I wish I still lived there with all my pleasant memories." Consequently I always used to advise the survivor to hold on if at all possible and if, after six months or maybe a year, he or she still wanted to sell, then do so. So soon after bereavement few people are in a fit state of mind to make such a major decision which is so often regretted later.'

'It is important to preserve independence for as long as possible. Again, subject to the overriding considerations of health and finances, I used to advise widows/widowers to live in their own home for as

long as they could manage it without neglecting themselves. Independence, in my experience, was one of the key factors of the bereaved surviving for a long time. Once they become totally dependent on someone else they often tend to let go, with the inevitable result.'

Some people cope with the death of a loved one by throwing themselves into punishing work schedules or frenetic activity. It helps them push the pain that they are feeling to the back of their thoughts, but sooner or later that pain must be expressed.

'Having to contend with the pressures of everyday living makes one feel more capable. A sense of loneliness is inevitable, but aloneness takes its place, and one can begin to enjoy that.'

'Nights are awful. I prepared for a siege. Biscuit, apple, magazines, and wish somebody had told me about all - night radio. Do prepare for bedtime earlier in the evening. Make the room feel welcoming by turning the light on, wearing pretty nightwear.'

'In the numbing first few weeks, give yourself a very small goal every day. Straighten a picture, sew on a button, anything simple enough to be achievable – and then praise yourself loud and long.'

It is also a good idea to think through the things you always wanted to do but did not because your partner had no interest in them. Now is the time to try. *'You must develop your* resources to the full.'

Whether you want to sing, dance, or tap your troubles away, there are groups doing just that not further than the columns of your local paper. What about the picture you wanted to paint, the countries you wanted to visit? 'Push to the back of your mind that it is the riches of an insurance policy that now enables you to do it– just go.'

In every small town there is something going on outside the front door. However mundane it may seem at first, 'Whatever new you do leads to new friends,' and if you do not get out, 'No one will come looking for you.' Even if you are not very good at making conversation, always remember a smile is the start of one. It can also lead to an equally lonely new friend.

However awful and unfeeling it sounds, life does go on, and in time you will find yourself hurting slightly less. You will not ever forget, and life will never ever be the same again, but in order to survive, you adapt.

One women wrote:

'A cousin said to me, "Be kind to yourself." For over a year into my widowhood, I had occasional lapses into guilt and self-doubt, but since then my practical resourcefulness seems to have been sharp-

ened, through the sheer need to survive alone.'

Another wrote:

'Bereavement affects people in all different ways. For me, the first year I felt in a state of shock and I got through it by keeping busy. The second year I found harder, because by then you have realised this has happened and have to come to terms with it and rebuild your life. Keeping busy is the best medicine, and at the moment my goal is to swim a mile.'

'Losing someone you love has made us a very close family and has made me realise how important life is, and I feel it has made me into a more caring and thoughtful person.'

A woman who lost both her mother and father wrote:

'My personality changed. I seemed to envy all my friends who still had their parents and I became very bitter; but now, although I still miss Mum and Dad and the pain doesn't really ease, I'm easier to live with and I've got my confidence back. I would say I'm a stronger person than I was before. Life is too precious to sit and mope about, but it's taken me nearly four years to come to terms with everything. People should realise when they say, "Oh, you should be over it by now," that it's just not that easy and it takes however long it takes!'

Death: the human condition

The Rev. Ian M. Ainsworth-Smith, Chaplain, St George's Hospital, Tooting

Some years ago I was talking with a patient in the hospital where I work. He was facing death in the form of an illness which was slowly destroying his nervous system and which meant an end to his professional life as a doctor. The illness was making deep inroads into his personal life, affecting even such basic elements as movement and simple speech. He had heard that I was attempting to write about the pastoral care of people who were facing their own death and of people who were bereaved. I shall never forget how he asked me whether we had given space in the book to what he called the 'little deaths'. 'Please tell them,' he said, 'of the time when I first realised that I could not hold my hand still. Then later, when I realised that I could no longer drive, nor get upstairs by myself. Those little deaths,' he said 'seemed every bit as important and painful as the actual death which I am facing.'

It is easy to think of death as some-thing which is a 'one-off' event just involving the cessation of breathing, when for many people there is so much else involved. Indeed, thinking about the 'little deaths' may throw other important losses into some sort of perspective. I have worked with the carers who have looked after handicapped relatives. They speak poignantly of being with a person physically when the person they have known and loved is no longer there in any real sense. Much research has recently been done on those losses which seem to have the highest risk for a person's psychological well-being. This research suggests that, for example, the loss of a partner through divorce or separation counts as seriously as the loss of a partner through death. So there is more to facing death, including our own, than just the fact of physical death.

In the Christian tradition – and in other religious and philosophical traditions too – death is frequently thought of as one of the 'last' things in life, not in the sense of it being a final event but of discovering a thread which runs right through life in which 'last' means acknowledging the nearness and reality of death and loss as a dimension against which life can be lived more fully.

To take a view of death which is integrated with life is not always easy. In some historical periods preoccupation with death and seeing death as a punishment have been used as a morbid form of control, especially of children. One only needs to think of the number of Victorian children's books which have this theme. Equally, Lily Pincus in her book *Death in the Family* pointed out sensitively and clearly that 'the children of parents who fear death will fear life.'

This raises the issue of how often groups of people – children, people who are seen as mentally handicapped or mentally ill, and the elderly – may often be shielded from the reality of death in what is seen as 'their own interests'. But the real issue seems to be the inability of many people who are not in these categories to talk honestly with people who may be seen as vulnerable or 'different', when they may have much to give. My own experience, for example, of talking to many adults who have been bereaved as children is that it is not the experience of the bereavement which is remembered with most pain, but the sense of exclusion,

knowing that something was going on but not being part of it, and therefore wondering whether, at some level not properly understood but deeply felt, they were responsible for what had happened.

Equally, death can be denied and avoided with results that can be bizarre and morbid. There is a large multi-million- pound teaching hospital which went several stages into its planning and development before anyone noticed that the plans did not include a mortuary. Yet the majority of people do die in hospital nowadays. Even there, however, the realities of death can be 'fudged' by euphemisms like 'he has passed away' or 'we lost her in the night' or by practices such as drawing bed curtains when a body is removed, ostensibly to protect the feelings of patients and relatives but frequently a way that hospital staff, who are the products of the same pressures as everyone else, can minimise their own anxieties.

We may be asked to believe that fantasy is a kind thing to offer a bereaved person and that the reality may destroy them. I believe quite the reverse is the case. When I studied a group of people who had been bereaved, I found that six months later the vast majority of those who had not been given the opportunity to see the body had very much regretted the lost opportunity, whereas a very small minority had regretted

DEATH: THE HUMAN CONDITION

having seen it.

There is also very clear research evidence that very many people who are dying seem to know it. Many may not choose to acknowledge the fact to themselves or to tell anyone else in words, but it is dangerous to imagine that things unspoken mean that the dying person is unaware of the true facts. I remember one terminally ill man who was very anxious to save his wife distress since she had a number of personal problems and he did not want her to know how ill he was. Some weeks later I met the wife who told me how relieved she was that he had never known how sick he was.

There is a real difference, too, between talking about death at an intellectual level and coming to terms with its reality. The philosopher Kirkegaard tells the parable of a scholar who had proved conclusively that the soul survives after death; however, on his way to give his learned dissertation to a scholarly society he met Death and had to run away, since his arguments were locked up in his briefcase.

The need to be helpful and to 'do something' can be very strong and, of course, there is a time when this is right. But so often there may be a very thin line between the need to help and the need to control the situation in the face of death, since everyone involved may have to face

their own feeling of helplessness and the need to say or do something which may magically make things better. It can be all right to say that there is nothing to say. The religious and philosophical language which we use about dying and bereavement, if it is to be helpful, needs to connect with the experience rather than abdicate from it.

The experience of all of us who work with dying people is that there are so often occasions when one really wonders who is doing the caring, since dying people so often have much to give and may become deeply frustrated if they are constantly 'done to' by other people.

I remember being brought up short in my early attempts to support a dying person when my nervousness and verbosity became all too apparent. The other person patted my hand and said quietly, 'It's all right, dear.' Indeed, giving up being a person who is seen as having something to give and becoming a 'patient' or labelled as 'terminally ill' is often one of the most difficult of the 'little deaths' I mentioned earlier. But living close to dying and to a dying person can, with proper support, give ordinary events a very special sort of quality because the usual considerations just do not apply and it may be possible to make every moment count in a very special way.

I recently spent an evening with two friends, a husband and wife. She was clearly dying and was aware of it. I remember the evening as rich and enjoyable, just because everybody present knew the reality, did not deny it, and was able to enjoy the evening to the full just because so much had been acknowledged. In the same way the ability to laugh and to cry properly are more closely linked than one might imagine.

Although intellectually we know it is not so, most of us think that death is going to come at the very end of life and that tragedies are more likely to happen to somebody else. The effect of illness or sudden tragedy is to breach those very natural and understandable human defences so that those things which are 'out there' are seen to have happened to people 'just like ourselves'. I was recently involved in the team care of patients, relatives and staff after a major accident in which my hospital was involved. Talking things over as a group of staff, we agreed that one of the most difficult things to cope with was that the tragedy had overtaken so many people who were so similar to ourselves and going about everyday, normal things. We had all encountered sudden tragedies in the course of our work before but on a smaller scale. We agreed that the experience had affected us more than we had anticipated, and that we were never going to be the same again.

Facing death means that one needs to explore the question of the very important difference between feeling depressed (which, for me, means being empty of feeling) and feeling and expressing sadness, which is very normal but is often not properly part of facing any sort of loss. (When I ask the question of people I work with, very few can remember many positive experiences of being sad from their childhood. More often they remember equating understandable sadness with self-indulgence.) Talk of 'cheering up' or 'putting a brave face on it' can mean that a dying or bereaved person is put under intolerable stress to be something which they are not but which they come to believe is the only face acceptable to other people.

That is why the idea of letting go is so important when attempting to make sense of the human face of dying and bereavement. Both the dying person and those close to them have to let go of future plans, their picture of the world as a safe and consistent place and, eventually, life. That sounds easy, but of course involves taking enormous risks. There is no evidence that suffering automatically makes people better. Everything depends on how much the person is helped and is able to make something of the experience. It was well put for me by a patient who was dying who asked me, 'I can't believe, but can I hope?' Facing death and bereavement involves constantly reorganising and redefining what one means by 'hope'. At one point it may mean the removal of the symptoms; at another the relief of pain; at another the putting right of a relationship; at another thinking that love has a future as well as a past and a present. It also involves balancing two opposite and important views of life. These are best summarised by a farmer's epitaph on the wall of a country church: 'Farm as if you are going to farm for a thousand years. Live as if you are going to die tomorrow.'

Helpful organisations

Before contacting any of the voluntary organisations listed here, it is worth first of all checking locally – your doctor, local health centre, the social services department of your local council or Citizens' Advice Bureau – whose addresses you will find in your local telephone directories. Any of these should have an extensive and detailed knowledge of what help is available in your area and may well be able to put you in contact with many organisations not listed here, particularly the more specialised or localised ones.

If you do contact any of the following organisations directly for further information about their objectives and services, please bear in mind that most depend on voluntary donations to survive and would greatly appreciate you enclosing a stamped addressed envelope if you are writing, and possibly even a small donation.

From 6 May 1990 the telephone numbers of organisations based in London will change to the ones shown in brackets.

Help for the dying and their carers

HOSPICE INFORMATION SERVICE

51–59 Lawrie Park Road
Sydenham
London SE26 6DZ
Tel: 01-778 9252   (081-778 9252)

Although admission to a hospice is usually made through your local or hospital doctor, St Christopher's Hospice in London runs a national information service.

CANCER RELIEF MACMILLAN FUND

Anchor House
15–19 Britten Street
London SW3 3TZ
Tel: 01-351 7811   (071-351 7811)

Supports and develops services to provide skilled care and improve the quality of life for people with cancer and their carers. Macmillan nurses are specially trained in pain and symptom control and emotional support. Macmillan cancer care units provide in-patient and day care. Financial help is given through grants. Referrals for Macmillan nursing services should be made through your doctor or community nurse. Applications for grants should be made through community nurses, hospital or local authority social workers.

MARIE CURIE CANCER CARE

28 Belgrave Square
London SW1X 8QG
Tel: 01-235 3325   (071-235 3325)

Provides nursing care for people with cancer through 11 in-patient Marie Curie Community Homes (359 beds) throughout the UK, and through 4,800 Marie Curie Community Nurses to care for cancer patients in their own homes. This service is free to the patient and is available through the Nursing Manager (Community) in the local health authority. For further information, please contact the organisation at the above telephone number.

BACUP: BRITISH ASSOCIATION OF CANCER UNITED PATIENTS

121-123 Charterhouse Street
London EC1M 6AA

Cancer Information Service:
For London call :
01 608 1661 (071 608 1661)
(10 am-7 pm Mon-Thur)
(10 am-5.30 pm Fridays)
Outside London call the Freeline on: 0800 181 199

Aims to provide cancer patients and their families and friends with a free, confidential cancer information and support service.

CANCERLINK

17 Britannia Street
London WC1X 9JN
Tel: 01-833 2451 (071-833 2451)

Aims to provide people with cancer, their relatives and friends with support and information about cancer. It can also provide information about local cancer self- help and support groups and has produced a directory of these groups.

THE TERRENCE HIGGINS TRUST

52–54 Grays Inn Road
London WC1X 8JU
Tel: 01-242 1010 (071-242 1010)
Helpline 3-10 pm. every day

Aims to provide welfare, legal and counselling help and support to people with AIDS and related conditions, and to their friends and families.

MEDICAL ADVISORY SERVICE

10 Barley Mow Passage
Chiswick
London W4 4PH
Tel: 01-994 9874 (081-994 9874)
(10 am – 10 pm Monday to
Friday)

A telephone service, run by nurses, offering advice on medical and health - care matters, putting people in touch with the right organisations.

CARERS NATIONAL ASSOCIATION

29 Chilworth Mews
London W2 3RG
Tel: 01-724 7776 (071-724 7776)

Offers information, advice, support and opportunities for self-help to: carers of the disabled, elderly or dying; carers who have recently been bereaved. Helps them to know what is available in terms of benefits and services and refers them to other organisations.

CROSSROADS: ASSOCIATION OF CROSSROADS CARE ATTENDANT SCHEMES

94 Coton Road
Rugby
Warwickshire CV21 4LN
Tel: 0788-73653

Provides support for carers in their own homes.

Practicalities

NATIONAL ASSOCIATION OF FUNERAL DIRECTORS (NAFD)

618 Warwick Road
Solihull
West Midlands
B91 1AA
Tel: 021-711 1343

The governing body of the profession which also, through its members, runs a formal scheme for the prepayment of funeral expenses. A leaflet explaining their funeral expenses plan is available from any undertaker who is a member of the NAFD.

BODY: BRITISH ORGAN DONOR SOCIETY

Balsham
Cambridge CB1 6DL
Tel: 0223-893636

Self- help and support group for families of organ donors and for those who have received organs. They will also welcome calls from people waiting to receive organs. The society is run by voluntary help. There is a 24- hour answerphone when the office is closed, or there is no one available to speak.

If the deceased has asked that their body be donated for medical research, arrangements should have been made for this. For further information and forms contact:

HM inspector of Anatomy
Department of Health
Portland Court
158–176 Great Portland Street
London W1N 5TB
Tel: 01-872 9302 (071-872 9302)

For those in the London area, phone the London Anatomy Office on 01-387 7850 (071-387 7850).

Social Security

As well as leaflets (see appendix 2: Further reading), you can receive information by dialling 0800-66655, the free social security telephone information service.

Support for the bereaved

The following are some of the many organisations which offer bereavement counselling services or can provide information on local groups who do. Many are able to offer practical advice as well as support and comfort.

AGE CONCERN (England)

60 Pitcairn Road
Mitcham
Surrey CR4 3LL

Tel: 01-640 5431 (081-640 5431)
Will be moving premises in June 1990

AGE CONCERN (Scotland)

54a Fountainbridge
Edinburgh EH3 9PT
Tel: 031- 228 5656

AGE CONCERN (Wales)

4th floor
1 Cathedral Road
Cardiff
Tel: 0222-371566

Age Concern has 1,400 independent local groups in the UK. It provides counselling as well as practical information for the elderly and a range of practical services with 250,000 volunteers.

THE BEREAVED PARENTS HELPLINE

6 Canon's Gate
Harlow
Essex
Tel: 0279-412745 or 0279-39685
(Jill and Alan Lodge)

The group works locally in the Harlow area, but is happy to talk to parents anywhere who have lost a child; they can refer elsewhere if necessary. Help is normally given on a one-to-one basis.

COMPASSIONATE FRIENDS

6 Denmark Street
Bristol BS1 5DQ
Tel: 0272-292778

A nationwide self-help organisation of parents whose child of any age, including adult, has died from any cause. Personal and group support are offered. A quarterly newsletter, postal library and a range of leaflets are offered. A befriending, not a counselling, service.

CRUSE–BEREAVEMENT CARE

Cruse House
126 Sheen Road
Richmond
Surrey TW9 1UR
Tel: 01-940 4818   (081-940 4818)

Cruse provides a service of counselling, advice and opportunities for social-contact to all bereaved people.

THE NATIONAL ASSOCIATION OF WIDOWS

54–57 Allison Street
Digbeth
Birmingham B5 5TH
Tel: 021-643 8348

With branches throughout the country, it offers friendly support, information and advice to all widows and those concerned to help widows overcome the many problems they face in society today.

THE SAMARITANS

Tel: consult your telephone directory or Yellow Pages

Runs local helplines throughout the country for those feeling suicidal or in despair.

Other specialist bereavement counselling services

GAY BEREAVEMENT PROJECT

Unitarian Rooms
Hoop Lane
London NW11 8BS
Tel: 01-455 8894   (081-455 8894)

An answerphone message gives the telephone number of a person you can talk to between 7.00 pm and midnight every day.

FOUNDATION FOR BLACK BEREAVED FAMILIES

11 Kingston Square
Salters Hill
London SE19 1JE
Tel: 01-761 7228   (081-761 7228)
Contact: Lorreene Hunte

National organisation offering advice and support to black bereaved families. Moving premises in mid– 1990.

THE FOUNDATION FOR THE STUDY OF INFANT DEATHS

(Cot Death Research and Support)
35 Belgrave Square
London
SW1X 8QB
Tel: 01-235 0965 (071-235 0965)
or 01-235 1721 (071-235 1721)
weekdays 9.00 am–5.00 pm.
Answerphone 01-235 1721
(071-235 1721) outside office
hours.

Raises funds for research into the causes and prevention of cot deaths, acts as a centre for information for both parents and health professionals and gives personal support to bereaved parents by letter, telephone and leaflets. It also puts parents in touch with groups of previously – bereaved parents – Friends of the Foundation, who offer an individual befriending service.

HEART LINE ASSOCIATION

40 The Crescent
Briket Wood
St Albans
Hertfordshire AL2 3NF
Tel: 0923-670763 (Val Kane)

Mutual support group for parents of children with heart disease. They have a newly formed bereavement support group.

JEWISH BEREAVEMENT COUNSELLING SERVICE

1 Cyprus Gardens
London N3 1SP
Tel: 01-349 0839 (081-349 0839), answerphone at times
or 01-387 4300 (071-387 4300) ext. 227 during office hours.

Offers counselling in the homes of bereaved families in north-west and south-west London. Outside this area they may be willing to arrange a meeting at a mutually convenient location.

THE MISCARRIAGE ASSOCIATION

P.O. Box 24
Ossett
West Yorkshire WF5 8XG
Tel: 0924-830515

Provides information and support for women and their families both during and after miscarriage. Support groups have been organised throughout the country. The answerphone message gives names and telephone numbers of people who can tell you who is your local contact.

NATIONAL ASSOCIATION OF BEREAVEMENT SERVICES

68 Charlton Street
London NW1 1JR
Tel: 01-388 2153 (071-388 2153)

This newly formed association

aims to compile a directory of all existing bereavement services throughout the UK, to act as a resource not only for bereaved individuals and families but for anyone in the field seeking information and advice. LONDON BEREAVEMENT PROJECT GROUP is based at the same address, and with the same phone number as the entry above. They act as a co-ordinating body for small community-based bereavement services throughout London.

PARENTS OF MURDERED CHILDREN SUPPORT GROUP

Compassionate Friends
46 Winters Way
Waltham Abbey
Essex EN9 3HP
Tel: 0992-760342,
Contact: Jill Palm

A group within Compassionate Friends for parents of murdered children. Members help each other by listening compassionately, sharing feelings and experiences and being supportive,

particularly at traumatic times such as a trial.

THE STILLBIRTH AND NEONATAL DEATH SOCIETY (SANDS)

28 Portland Place
London W1N 4DE
Tel: 01-436 5881   (071-436 5881)
You can call the SANDS telephone support service at any time. During office hours (9.30 am –5.00 pm) there will always be someone to talk to you. At all other times, a recorded message gives two emergency telephone numbers to phone.

VOLUNTARY EUTHANASIA SOCIETY

13 Prince of Wales Terrace
London W8 5PG
Tel: 01-937 7770 (071-937 7770)

Pressure group whose principle aim is to make it legal for an adult person, who is suffering distress from an incurable illness, to receive medical help to die, at their own considered request.

Further reading

There are many more books written about this subject than we can include in this list, but we have listed just a few titles of books that you might wish to consult.

All in the End Is Harvest: An Anthology for Those who Grieve, edited by Agnes Whitaker. Darton, Longman and Todd in association with CRUSE, 1985. ISBN: 0-232-51624-3

Can I Forget You? Coping with Widowhood by Pamela Winfield. Constable 1987. ISBN: 0-09-467890-1

Caring at Home: A Handbook for People Looking after Someone at Home by Nancy Kohner. National Extension College, 1988. ISBN: 1-85356-004-9

The Courage to Grieve by Judy Tatelbaum. Heinemann, 1981. ISBN: 0-434-75650-4

Death Be not Proud by Peter Mullen. Fount Paperbacks: Collins, 1989. ISBN: 0-00-627467-6

Dying by John Hinton. Penguin, 1967 (2nd edn,1972). ISBN: 0-1402-0866-6

Facing Death by C. M. Parkes. National Extension College, 1980. ISBN: 1-85356-028-6

I Don't Know What to Say: How to Help and Support Someone who is Dying by Dr Robert Buckman. Papermac: Macmillan, 1988. ISBN: 0-333-46983-6

Letting Go: Caring for the Dying and Bereaved by Ian Ainsworth-Smith and Peter Speck. SPCK, 1982 (7th impression, 1988). ISBN: 0281-038619

Living while Dying by Dr R. Glyn Owens and Freda Naylor. Thorsens, 1989. ISBN 0-7225-1620-7

On Death and Dying by Elisabeth Kubler Ross. Tavistock Publications, 1970. ISBN: 0-422-75490-0

Tears and Smiles: The Hospice Handbook by Martyn Lewis. Michael O'Mara Books , 1989. ISBN: 1-85479-060-9

Tomorrow Who Knows? by Alma and Ray Moore. Constable, 1989. ISBN: 0-09-469370-6

What to Do when Someone Dies by Which? Books. Consumers' Association, 1967 (revised 1986). ISBN: 0-340-39963-5 and 0-85202-338-3

Wills and Probate by Which? Books. Consumers' Association, 1988. ISBN: 0-85202-393-6 and 0-340-48604-X

LEAFLETS

Official government leaflets are usually available from the Registrar's office, the local Social Security office, your local post office or from:

Leaflets Unit
P.O. Box 21
Stanmore
Middlesex HA7 1AY

The Department of Social Security Leaflet D49– *What to Do after a Death: A guide to what you must do and the help you can get* - is free and contains much essential, important and useful information covering many different areas as well as details of other leaflets available covering benefits, pensions and taxes. There is a special version available in Scotland.